GIRO d'ITALIA

THE STORY OF THE WORLD'S MOST BEAUTIFUL BIKE RACE

COLIN O'BRIEN

This revised paperback edition published in 2018

First published in Great Britain in 2017 by
PURSUIT BOOKS
an imprint of Profile Books Ltd
3 Holford Yard
Bevin Way
London
WC1X 9HD

www.profilebooks.com

1 3 5 7 9 10 8 6 4 2

Designed and typeset by sue@lambledesign.demon.co.uk
Printed and bound in Great Britain by
CPI Group (UK) Ltd, Croydon CR0 4YY

A CIP catalogue record for this book is available from the
British Library.

ISBN 978 1 78125 717 3
eISBN 978 1 78283 290 4

CONTENTS

PREFACE

With the possible exception of a long Christmas dinner at home in Dublin, there's nothing I look forward to every year more than the Giro d'Italia. There are a few reasons for this: first, the route tends to take the race, and with it the journalists, to a great many places that I would never otherwise see. And second, after having had my appetite whetted by the early season's one-day classics, the promise of three weeks of continuous, ever-changing, unpredictable action never fails to fire the imagination. But more than that, I look forward to the Giro because it heralds the arrival of summer. The weather in May is still capricious, and the mountains still covered in snow, but once you see the pink of the Maglia Rosa you know that long, sun-drenched days are not far off.

There's also the social aspect to it. The Giro is something to talk about. Like football, but less formulaic. The race's history is littered with riders who were nailed-on to win it, right up until the moment when they didn't, and that keeps it interesting, making every edition feel new. It helps, too, that the race is the real attraction. More than the teams or the riders, you tune in or turn up to see the Giro itself. Without wanting to trivialise its ability to excite and entertain, the Giro is just something to do. For the guts of a month every year, it ingrains itself into everyday life in a way that few other cultural phenomena can. It can be joyful, heart-breaking, exhilarating and infuriating. It can be all those things at once. But it is rarely, if ever, boring. If anyone asks me why they should watch it, that's the reason I give. It's also the best reason I had to write this book.

Obviously, this is a work of non-fiction, but from the outset I had an overarching narrative in mind. The deeper I went with my research, the more tempting it became to deviate from that idea and mention every single detail of the race's 108-year history, but it was never my intention to write an encyclopaedia of the Giro d'Italia, because I would never want to read one. I wanted to tell the story of what I think is the world's most exciting sporting event. I hope that this book does it justice.

INTRODUCTION

Imagine a different Italy. A recently integrated kingdom of disparate regions, mostly inhabited by peasantry. Almost half the population was illiterate, and the majority spoke dialect rather than the Florentine standard of the state. Even the country's first king, Victor Emmanuel II, Padre della Patria, Father of the Fatherland, struggled to use the country's official language.

What roads existed were rough and narrow and rarely, if ever, paved. Away from the cobbled urban centres, mostly they were nothing more than compacted dirt and gravel. The masses relied on mules and bicycles, not cars, for labour and transport. The Fabbrica Italiana Automobili Torino (Fiat), was less than a decade old and some way away from becoming one of Europe's great automotive giants. Rome, Milan, Turin and Naples were all experiencing rapid growth, but the majority of the country's 32 million inhabitants lived in small towns or in the countryside.

The capital was still plagued by malaria from the dreaded Pontine Marshes, and it would be 20 years before the Italian government resolved its dispute with the Vatican, having forcibly annexed the Papal States in 1870. Giuseppe Garibaldi, the general and politician who was born in Nice but would go on to lead the Risorgimento, Italy's unification, had only died 27 years ago. The country was rapidly changing, and the Giro d'Italia was both a reflection, and a reaction, to that fact. The founding fathers' desire to build a modern state, the creation of the Kingdom of Italy and the attempted integration of its diverse, remote and often contradictory constituent parts, was still more current affairs than ancient history when the race's first edition rolled away from the *Gazzetta dello Sport*'s office on Milan's Piazzale Loreto in 1909. As strange and as modern a contraption as the bicycle must have seemed to many onlookers, the very idea of having an 'Italy' to ride around was most likely just as intriguing a curiosity.

Cycling fans in the Bel Paese sometimes joke that the race has done more to unite Italy than Garibaldi's Risorgimento ever managed. And while this is said with tongue planted firmly in cheek, perhaps there's a grain of truth to it, because in the early twentieth century this was still very much a country divided. Much of the north was against integration, as was the Vatican, and while Naples and the south supported it, that had more to do with disdain for the Bourbon royal family and the Kingdom of the Two Sicilies than it did with any real enthusiasm for the new state. 'L'Italia è fatta. Restano da fare gli italiani,' observed Massimo d'Azeglio, the prime minister of Sardinia and a supporter of unification. 'Italy has been made. Now we must make Italians.'

It would be hard not to notice a certain irony in the effect that the country's peculiar geography has on its citizens and their relationship with the nation, even today in an age of motorways, high-speed rail and low-cost flights. Because while it was never very useful when it came to discouraging foreign encroachment, Italy's topography – from the great plains of the north, bounded by the Alps and the Dolomites, to the long, narrow peninsula that is almost completely bisected by the Apennines – has been very effective in keeping its own inhabitants separate and ensconced in their own cultural, culinary and linguistic idiosyncrasies. Even if you arrived blindfolded to a town, a simple look at a local menu would give you an idea of where you were. In our age of convenience, you might find a cuttlefish risotto in Florence or Milan, but it won't compare to Venetian archetype. Tortellini are best eaten in Emilia-Romagna, and pizza in Naples. Turin is veal braised in red wine, and powerful cheeses with a clear French influence. Orecchiette, little pasta discs named after the 'little ears' they resemble, mean Puglia, and you're unlikely to find a plate of Pajata, the intestines of an unweaned calf, or a truly special carbonara, outside of the capital. Even something as simple as the Sicilian arancini – deep-fried rice balls traditionally stuffed with a meat sauce and peas – can give a little locational hint, because they change shape from spherical to conical depending on whether you're on the north or the south coast of the island.

Italy is a land of inconsistencies and complications. No one who's ever spent any time here will describe it as easy, and yet, that's part of the charm. It's also a huge part of the Giro's soul, because unlike the Tour de France, which can sometimes seem prosaic and anaemic in its homogeny, the Italian event is a chaotic, unabashed celebration of the country's colourful, often schizophrenic personality. You can be in the cramped, crumbling streets of Naples one day and at altitude at an Apennine ski resort the next. The grand boulevards and Baroque piazzas of Turin can follow the snow-capped Alps or the verdant, craggy coastline of Liguria and the Costa Azzurra. The bustling, beating heart of Milan, the country's business capital, can quickly give way to the agrarian, pan-flat expanses of the Pianura Padana, and the captivating cities of the once mighty maritime Venetian republic – Venice, Padova, Verona, Vicenza, Treviso – often herald the race's impending arrival among the dramatic peaks of the Dolomite mountain range.

The Giro isn't the biggest race in professional cycling, but in the eyes of many fans and a lot of riders, it is the most beautiful – and difficult – grand tour. Because unlike the Tour, which is often formulaic, and dominated by the strongest, richest teams, the Giro is unpredictable and capricious. An abundance of choice means that the route is always original and fresh, and in contrast with the Tour, even the most iconic climbs can go through long periods of inactivity while the organisers look elsewhere for something novel. The springtime climate coupled with the Giro's predilection for callous climbs and technical descents means that the race tends to reward the rider who takes the biggest risks. You don't win a Giro by riding conservatively – you have to grab it by the scruff of the neck. In many ways, it's a race for the purists. The route is more difficult, the terrain more varied, the weather more changeable, and the racing less controllable. And a strong Italian presence in the peloton always ensures that local pride plays a role, which is why you often see hard-to-fathom breakaways and incredibly emotional victory salutes. If the race passes by a rider's home, you better believe he is going to put on a show. And though the crowds don't always compare to those found at the roadside during the Tour, the Italian tifosi are more passionate and knowledgeable, because even in the twenty-first century, as road cycling becomes ever more globalised, Italy remains its heartland. Many of the sport's most iconic brands hail from the peninsula, and legends like Gino Bartali, Fausto Coppi, Felice Gimondi, Francesco Moser and Marco Pantani continue to inspire. Italians still make up the majority of the professional peloton, and amateur riders come from all over the globe to ride iconic climbs like Stelvio, Gavia, Mortirolo, Zoncolan, Tre

Cime di Lavaredo, Colle di Finestre, Giau, and Monte Grappa.

The first edition of the Giro was an audacious publicity stunt, cobbled together on the fly by a handful of ambitious young journalists at the *Gazzetta dello Sport*, but more on that later. A lot has happened in the subsequent 108 years. It has grown from an eight-stage war of attrition, where brute endurance was the order of the day, to a 21-stage battle of wits and tactics, played out at breakneck speed. It waited until 1950 for its first foreign winner, the charismatic and hugely popular Swiss rider Hugo Koblet, but has since become an incredibly pluralistic and international event, without ever losing its indelible Italian character. During the sport's golden age, the romance of the rivalry between Bartali and Coppi captivated the entire country and in some ways still influences how Italians view the sport in the twenty-first century. The enmity that characterised the relationship between Moser and Giuseppe Saronni, decades after Coppi and Bartali, still occasionally spills over even though they are both now in their sixties, and the controversy over Stephen Roche's 1987 Maglia Rosa still has the power to whip stubborn supporters of his teammate and rival, Roberto Visentini, into a rage.

On top of creating sporting legends, the race has also become entwined with political and commercial life in Italy. It's been used by governments as a propaganda tool, embroiled in the machinations of the Catholic Church and the Mafia, and exploited by many an entrepreneurial soul looking to gain exposure for their business ventures. Bicycle brands have built fortunes from Giro success, and with almost four million readers in print and online, the *Gazzetta*'s position as Italy's most-read daily owes much to the race, even if football has since taken over from cycling in the hearts of most sports fans. One famous example of what the Giro can do for a business is that of Romano Cenni's Mercatone Uno, a relatively small, regional supermarket chain that sponsored Marco Pantani's team. Riding the wave of Pantani-mania that swept Italy at the turn of the last century, Cenni has openly credited the diminutive climber's popularity with the proliferation of his shops across the country. Cenni even built a monument to him outside the company's headquarters in Imola.

After Pantani, the Giro went through a difficult time that was marred by doping scandals and declining public interest, as cycling seemed to become more like a science lesson than a sporting competition. In recent years, however, the race has been enjoying a renaissance and is beginning to crawl out from under the shadow of the Tour to be seen by the wider global public as one of the world's most important sporting events and an idiosyncratic highlight of the calendar in its own right, rather than just an Italian precursor to the main event across the border. The 2016 edition had a total audience of 827 million people in 194 countries, across more than 5,500 hours of dedicated television coverage. More than 500 of those hours were in Italy alone, and on the penultimate stage, some 3.6 million Italians – more than a quarter of the country's total TV viewers at that time – tuned in to watch the action unfold. Around 12.5 million turned out on the roadside to see the *Corsa Rosa* – the Pink Race is a common nickname for the Giro in Italy – pass by. And over the course of the race, around 2,000 journalists produced more than 46,000 articles. The organisation booked a total of 17,500 rooms over the course of the event for teams, officials, guests and some members of the press. And because this is the social media age, it would be remiss not to mention the 50 million tweets recorded during the month of May. With its idiosyncratic character, complex history and huge cast of characters, the Giro can sometimes seem to elude full comprehension, but it means a great deal to an awful lot of people. This book sets out to explore why that is.

1

THE GIRO IS BORN

In a manner perfectly fitting for cycling, the Giro d'Italia was inspired by a mixture of enmity, chance, cunning and risk. Sport had very little to do with it. Not in the pure, Corinthian sense, anyway, because fundamentally, the Giro was born to sell newspapers.

Whereas these days we associate the media with reportage and opinion, reaction to recent events and rumination on things soon to come, the nineteenth-century press tended to take a far more hands-on approach to filling column inches, whether through the serialisation of fiction or the staging of attention-grabbing events, such as the sponsorship of Hattie and Darwin McIlrath on their three-year, cycling circumnavigation of the globe by Chicago's *Inter-Ocean* newspaper in the late 1890s.

European newspapers had been experimenting with bicycle racing as a way to drive sales for some time before either the Tour de France or the Giro took shape. Across the border in France, *Le Vélocipède Illustré* was the first publication to turn to cycling in search of increased circulation, staging a race between Paris and Rouen in November 1869. The route was 123 kilometres from the capital, north along the Seine, and it attracted some 120 riders, including two women. Curiously, the rulebook forbade the use of dogs and sails, in what might be seen as an early anticipation of the sport's predilection for cheating. City to city racing, and the papers that promoted it, flourished and several of these inceptive contests still feature prominently today, including the oldest extant race, the Milano–Torino, and three of the five monuments, namely: Liège–Bastogne–Liège, Paris–Roubaix and Milano–Sanremo. Controlling these spectacles guaranteed what the twenty-first-century media would call exclusive content, which in turn meant guaranteed sales.

It wasn't just the papers out to fill their pockets, either. If cycling wasn't the first sport to embrace commercialism, it was certainly number one when it came to pursuing it with unfettered, capitalistic zeal. Football, now the paragon of sporting avarice, was then an amateur affair, and in its infancy in Italy at the turn of the century, limited to a few clubs set up by British migrants in Genoa and Turin. Cycling was where the money was. Publishers loved it for its inherent promise of drama, and the tantalising mix of suffering and spectacle that attracted readers in their droves. Teams entered to sell bicycles, machines proven in the harshest of conditions and inextricably linked to the heroes who rode them. And riders flocked to the start-line for the promise of food and perhaps a bed, and for the remote hope of winning a fortune.

Just like those early riders, the nascent *Gazzetta dello Sport* in Milan was in dire need of cash. The earliest editions of the *Gazzetta* were a far cry from today's media behemoth. For a start, they were printed on green paper, rather than the now iconic pink stock, which came in 1898. It was a combination of two smaller papers, both dedicated to cycling – *Il Ciclista* and *La Tripletta* – and it came out twice a week, on Monday and

Friday. When it first hit newsstands on 3 April 1986, there were just five people involved in its production and it was just four pages in total. The front page featured a now rather quaint-looking advertisement for a shop in Turin selling tyres and inner tubes.

On 5 August 1908, the *Gazzetta*'s editor, Tullo Morgagni, sent a brief telegram to his cycling correspondent Armando Cougnet, telling him to return to Milan at once. 'Without delay, necessity obliges the *Gazzetta* to launch an Italian tour.' Eugenio Camillo Costamagna, the paper's owner, got the same message and ended his holiday immediately. A conspiracy was brewing, and there was no time to waste.

Angelo Gatti, formerly of the Bianchi bicycle factory but now very much their rival, having set up his own business, Atala, in 1908, had been in touch with Morgagni, offering some very interesting information. Bianchi were planning a nation-wide cycle race with the Touring Club Italiano and the *Corriere della Sera* newspaper. Having seen what Henri Desgrange's Tour de France had done for his publication, *l'Auto*, and the swift manner in which it had allowed him to crush France's biggest daily and his biggest rival, *Le Vélo*, the *Gazzetta*'s editor had no wish to be caught off-guard. It was imperative that they beat their competitors to the punch, and stage a tour of their own, post-haste.

Morgagni and his confederates didn't lack enthusiasm, but organising a national race was easier said than done, especially since the *Gazzetta* was on the ropes financially. The *Corriere della Sera* was a bigger paper, and while the Touring Club Italiano no longer involved itself in cycling, it had a huge logistical advantage because it held motor races throughout Italy. One thing that the enterprise did have going for it, however, was Coug-net's experience. Though just 18 when he joined the staff in 1898, the Nice native was an expert on all things cycling and had already been involved with the paper's first forays into racing, the Giro di Lombardia and Milano–Sanremo. He'd also been to France to cover the Tour, and so understood better than anyone else just what would be required to create a Giro d'Italia.

Just weeks after Morgagni's compelling communiqué, the 24 August front page broadcast the paper's intention to hold a tour of Italy the following May, trumpeting proudly: 'The *Gazzetta dello Sport*, having followed the new glory of Italian cycling and created its renown, announces for next spring the first edition of the Giro d'Italia, one of the biggest, most ambitious, tests in international cycling.' It also promised 3,000 kilometres of racing and 25,000 lire of prizes.

They'd got one over on the *Corriere* – but in doing so they'd also put their necks on the chopping blocks. The 28-year-old Cougnet, who would continue as director of the race until 1948, was confident in his own abilities to organise a stage race, but their bombastic headline had written cheques that the *Gazzetta* was in no position to cash. To put the prize money in perspective, the paper's owner, Costamagna, earned 1,800 lire a year, which was a very generous salary for the time. Nonetheless, it wasn't unusual for him or his staff to take home pay packets that were somewhat light, depending on how well business was going, and yet they'd committed to a purse that would make the Giro the richest race in the world.

Once the adrenalin wore off, reality sank in and by September they'd decided to cancel the event before a wheel had even been turned. Were it not for a twist of fate, the Corsa Rosa might never have existed at all. As it turned out, one of the paper's investors, a powerful Milanese banker by the name of Primo Bongrani, was also the secretary of the Italian Olympic committee and a big cycling fan. Upon returning from the 1908 London Games, he heard of the race's plight and immediately stepped in, insisting that it go ahead and pledging his full support to the fundraising effort. Bongrani's theory was that they'd just need some momentum before offers came flooding in, and so he secured early backing from the Lancia motorcar company and the Sanremo Casino, which was already involved with cycling through the Milano–Sanremo, which had been dreamt up as a way to promote the seaside town as a luxury destination. The pledge of a gold medal from the Italian monarch gave the enterprise a royal sheen, and it wasn't long before the offers came rolling in. Impressively, Bongrani even convinced their rivals at the *Corriere* to commit to a 3,000 lire investment, the logic being that the offer would garner them positive publicity and allow them to take the moral high ground by their involvement in helping an opponent's floundering venture.

By March, the coffers were full, and the paper announced the full details of an eight-stage route that would traverse Italy, covering 2,500 kilometres in total. That was less than they'd originally advertised, but still a vast enough distance that it would have seemed unfathomable to the average Italian, who rarely if ever had the chance to leave their native parish.

Both amateurs and professionals were welcome to compete, and 127 riders were present at the maiden Grande Partenza. On 13 May 1909, the first stage of the Giro d'Italia left Milan's Piazzale Loreto at 2.53 a.m., on a gruelling, 397-kilometre slog south to Bologna. Rather than using total elapsed time to calculate the overall winner, as is now common, the Giro used a points system to work out the general classification, adding up the placings of each stage to find the rider with the lowest number of points. Before the advent of more modern communication technology, this system was a lot easier – not to say cheaper – to monitor, and as such made sense. From Bologna, the race continued south to Chieti, near the Adriatic coast, before heading to Naples and then back north to Rome, Florence, Genoa, and Turin, returning to Milan for the finale 17 days later. Unlike grand tours today, this allowed for rest days in between each stage, because otherwise the distances, an average of 306 kilometres per stage in the first edition, would have been impossible with the equipment and the road conditions of the day. In stark contrast to the huge publicity and support caravan that follows every modern stage race, just eight cars accompanied the riders in 1909, four from teams, two for the organisation and the jury, and two for the press. Checkpoints were set up near train stations and riders were photographed at the start and finish to minimise the risk of cheating – it seems that cycling has attracted nefarious chancers since day one – and the jurors and reporters transmitted information on the race back to Milan by telegram. Those updates were posted to the windows of shops in the city, where the masses could digest all the action. Those few fortunate Italians who had a telephone could call a special number for more reports – a novelty that must have been as incredible as smartphone updates were a century later.

Luigi Ganna and Giovanni Gerbi were by far the most famous riders to compete that year, although several high-profile French riders did defy their team bosses to cross the Alps and take part in the new race, including Tour winners Louis Trousselier and Lucien Petit-Breton. Ganna was a stone-mason before becoming a bike racer, and it is rumoured that he'd ridden 100 kilometres a day round-trip between his job and his home in Induno Olona, north of Milan in the province of Varese. In that context, the Giro must have seemed like a vacation. He came to the Giro having won Milano–Sanremo in the spring, and with an already impressive palmarès that included victory at Milano–Torino, podiums at the Giro di Lombardia and a fifth-place finish at the 1908 Tour. Gerbi, known as the Red Devil, was wildly popular with the *Gazzetta*'s readers, not only for his athletic ability but also because his

relaxed moral code was ripe for myth making. He was allegedly given his nickname by a furious priest after he rode right
into the middle of a religious procession, and it is said that
when, in the second Tour de France, the riders were attacked
by an angry mob, Gerbi, then a teenager, was one of few to
fight back. Never one to baulk at a challenge, he was an enduring figure in early Italian cycling history, riding his last Giro in
1932, aged 47. He won the first edition of the Giro di Lombardia in 1905, as well as Milano–Torino and a hat-trick of wins
at both the Giro del Piemonte and Roma–Napoli–Roma. But
for the most part, the peloton was a proletarian affair, composed of unemployed or desperately poor men in search of a
way to put food on the table. The majority had no aspirations
towards victory, but the promise of 300 lire just for finishing
was motivation enough because that sum was sufficient to
support a family for several months. These independents had
no sponsors or support, and only a fortunate few could afford
accommodation. Many slept rough, or in farm buildings and
abandoned houses. Theirs was a thankless existence, and it's
difficult to imagine how bad things must have been at home
to force them into that temporary existence of itinerancy and
great physical hardship.

Within two kilometres of the start, there was a huge pile-up,
allegedly caused by a child in the road. Most of the riders were
quickly on their way again but Gerbi, one of the favourites, was
left in distress. His wheel had been damaged in the fall, and he
had to ride back into town until he found a mechanic who'd
stayed open because of the huge crowds. Before long, he was
back with the rest of them – something that would have been
impossible at that time in the Tour, because Desgrange ruled in
France like a tyrant, and it was his opinion that a race had to be
almost impossible. As such, a rider should be able to look after
himself, and anyone who received assistance or spare parts

from a third party was automatically disqualified. In keeping with the Italian mentality, the Giro organisers were somewhat more flexible when it came to setting strict rules.

Ganna didn't escape incident on that opening stage either, and found himself left for dust by his adversaries when he flatted, around 70 kilometres from the finish. The 25-year-old was able to catch up when the peloton was held up by a passing train, but didn't have enough energy left to race for victory. Some 14 hours after leaving Milan, the honour of the Giro's first stage win went to the Roman Dario Beni, who was just 20. After the first few riders, heavy rain and huge crowds made guesswork of the jury's final placings.

Stage two brought more drama on the 376-kilometre route to Chieti. Petit-Breton was too badly hurt to start, and reports at the time alleged that Gerbi was so exhausted that he stopped along the way, found an accommodating family, and borrowed a bed so that he could rest for a while before setting off again. At the uphill finish, Ganna finished second to Giovanni Cuniolo, and took the overall lead. The third stage was the Giro's first real day in the mountains, crossing the Apennines that run along the peninsula's spine, to Naples. A combination of atrocious roads, debilitating climbs, and single-speed bikes that weighed 15 kilos led to a large number of abandonments, including the winner of the previous stage. And as if conditions weren't bad enough, reports from the day describe the race director Cougnet using a whip to control the enormous, frenzied crowds. The stage to Rome was sabotaged by fans, who littered the route with nails in order to slow unpopular riders, but Ganna survived the hilly ordeal to take the win in front of more than 20,000 spectators in the capital. In Florence, he repeated his success by riding solo into the city's velodrome, driving his supporters into such euphoria that they invaded the track and forced the race judges to finish the race before the final lap. Trousselier had been held up by a bad mechanical, and when he eventually rolled in 28th, it was clear that he was too far behind in the general classification to challenge. He duly retired, and both of the Tour de France champions who'd travelled to Italy were out of contention. Only Carlo Galetti stood a chance of denying Ganna his triumph now. The downhill race into Genoa narrowed the gap, as Galetti finished second to Giovanni Rossignoli, a place ahead of Ganna to narrow the GC gap to a single point.

In the penultimate stage, Cougnet was forced to invent an elegant solution to a most welcome, albeit taxing, problem. The maiden Giro was more popular than anyone had imagined, and despite starting in the dead of night, huge crowds were mobbing the riders at every departure. The answer was the now commonplace neutralised start – a non-competitive roll until the peloton was safely away from the cheering masses. The young director's attempts at dealing with the throngs in Turin were less successful. Upon hearing that there was a baker's strike planned in the city, as well as 50,000 fans expected to line the streets, the organisers moved the finish six kilometres – but forgot to tell their local officials. In a torrential hailstorm and a madding crowd, Ganna beat Rossignoli to the stage win and extended his lead over Galetti to three points, leaving it all to play for on the final stage to Milan. After two rest days in Turin, the final day's 206-kilometre dash was raced at full tilt. Ganna flatted twice, and would have surely been out of the running had officials not stopped the peloton while it tried to illegally pass through a closed level crossing. The finish-line was again moved – Cougnet had obviously chosen to ignore the previous stage's lesson – and police on horseback were dispatched to deal with the crowds, only to themselves inadvertently cause a huge pile-up. When the final sprint was finally classified after some debate, young Beni was awarded victory ahead of Galetti and Ganna, the latter subsequently crowned champion of the debut Giro d'Italia.

It was a prodigious achievement for Ganna, the ninth son of a peasant farmer. Originally, his family had been sceptical of his ambition, but upon seeing how much money their boy could earn, they quickly changed their minds. By the time of the first Giro he was being paid a princely 250 lire a month by Atala, which, added to his race winnings, amounted to 24,000 lire, incredible for 1909. He'd earned more than 5,000 just for the Giro – more or less a year's salary for a middle-class white-collar worker. Proving himself to be as capable with finances as he was with a bicycle, Ganna opened up a bicycle factory of his own in 1912, before creating his very own team. That first Giro was to be his only win at a grand tour, and though he'd race for another six years, Ganna was never able to recreate the highs of that incredible season. But though it might have been the apogee for its inaugural champion, for the Giro d'Italia, Morgagni, Costamagna and Cougnet, and for Italian cycling, the best was yet to come.

2

THE EARLY YEARS

Cougnet and co. were on to something. Luigi Ganna may have been the Giro's first champion, but it was clear in the summer of 1909 that the race was the real star, and that the *Gazzetta dello Sport*, as its master, was the biggest winner. Publishing every other day, when the riders rested, the pink paper had seen a huge swell in readership as nascent *tifosi* nationwide – this Italian term for sports fans comes from the Greek *typhos*, from the fever – were bitten by the cycling bug and eager to devour all the gory details of the previous day's racing. A young footballer, recently retired, by the name of Emilio Colombo was hired as the paper's full-time editor and charged with following every stage of the race personally in order to provide as much coverage and colour as possible – not all of it strictly factual – to feed the public's seemingly insatiable hunger for the race.

The first Giro's success emboldened the organisers, so the following spring's edition was duly increased from eight to ten stages, covering just under 3,000 kilometres. That made the average stage length slightly shorter than the inaugural edition, but six of the ten were still over 320 kilometres, and the first day's route was a gruelling 388 kilometres from Milan to Udine, a small city northeast of Venice not far from the modern border with Slovenia.

Of the 101 starters who began the race on 18 May, 16 failed to reach the opening day's end and only 20 would make it back to Milan three weeks later. But though these early Giri were certainly wars of attrition rather than tests of outright speed, it's still impressive that the winner covered the route in a little over 13 hours, averaging almost 30 kilometres per hour. The opening honours of the second edition went to the Milanese Ernesto Azzini, a hulk of a rider who would later that summer become the first Italian winner of a stage at the Tour de France before retiring into anonymity a decade later and dying of tuberculosis aged just 38. Right behind him that day in Udine was another native of Milan, the 27-year-old Carlo Galetti, who was about to become the Giro's first dominant force.

Italian sports journalists have always loved nicknames, the weirder the better, and while it's not something that's restricted to cycling – football's Roberto Baggio was known as 'Il Divin Codino', the Divine Ponytail – over the years it has become a common part of the sport. These days we have Vincenzo Nibali, the Shark of the Strait, named for the sea beside his native Messina; and Fabio Aru, called the Knight of the Four Moors, in reference to the Sardinian flag. The early Giri were all about Galetti, 'Il Scoiattolo dei Navigli', the Squirrel of the Canals, a moniker presumably inspired by his riding style and by the canals that criss-crossed the neighbourhood in Milan from which he came. Unlike the determined-looking Ganna, who wore a strong parting in his hair and had an athletic build, or Gerbi, whose deep-set eyes and tightly cropped hair gave him a sinister look, Galetti's thick-set frame and balding pate gave him the genial look of agreeable middle age. But then appearances, as everyone knows, can be deceiving. He'd been a printer before becoming a cyclist, and reports of the time describe an exactitude in his riding that reflected the demands of his previous profession. The former typesetter had taken his narrow loss in the 1909 Giro quite badly, and spent the intervening 12 months preparing for the next event with dogged determination.

The single-mindedness of his character was to serve Galetti well in the coming weeks, as dozens of riders retired from the race. Ganna, the defending champion, was out of contention after the first day due to a costly flat tyre that left him in 21st place. He focused on stage wins, taking three, and though Galetti was ostensibly also a rival, the pair teamed up with Eberardo Pavesi to make sure that the foreigners, and in particular Lucien Petit-Breton, did not have an easy time of it on Italian soil. He was a past winner of Milano–Sanremo, Paris–Tours, Paris–Brussels and a two-time champion of the Tour de France, and one of the sport's first stars, but because of the points system the Frenchman was already hopelessly behind by the third stage, with 15 to Galetti's five. Taking the hint, Petit-Breton promptly packed his bags and set course for his home in Brittany before the start of the fourth stage to Naples. By the end of that day, the second-placed Pierino Albini had also abandoned, meaning that, barring disaster, the Giro was won with five stages still to go. Galetti, Pavesi and Ganna greedily divided up the remaining victories, with the Squirrel comfortably ending up atop the podium back in Milan with a commanding lead of 28 points to 46 and 51, respectively.

The first five editions of the race were run on a points system, with the lowest aggregate score taking the general classification, just like the Tour de France. A stage win earned one point, second place two, and so on, until 50th place, after which point any miserable soul who rolled in would be awarded 51 points and left alone to consider their vocation. This was an understandable simplification, given the rudimentary technology of the day and the difficulty in keeping accurate timings for a disparate group of raggedy cyclists over huge distances, and on the whole it was fair enough. But it's impossible not to feel some sympathy for poor old Giovanni Rossignoli, who would have won the Giro twice had a stopwatch been used instead of the placings.

Galetti's second triumph began in Rome. Cougnet had decided to give the Giro a more southern feel for 1911, with the start and finish both held in Rome, in celebration of the 50th anniversary of King Victor Emmanuel II's declaration of the Italian state. The route headed north from the capital to Florence, Genoa and the Ligurian coast, before skirting through Piemonte to Turin and on to Lombardy and Milan, from where it headed south to Bologna, Ancona, Abruzzo and Bari, looping up through Naples on its way back to the Eternal City.

Rossignoli gallantly fought the reigning champion in the opening stages and even held the lead for the first five days before Galetti took control. Petit-Breton, back over the border for more punishment, was also in the mix, becoming the first foreigner to lead the Giro's general classification when he snuck up on the duelling Italian duo to snatch the GC on stage nine to Sulmona, deep in the Apennines. The French star's luck wouldn't hold, however, and a crash forced him to retire on stage 11, cruelly just two points off Galetti at the top of the leader board. For the second year in a row, the Milan native was all conquering. And for the second time in three years, Rossignoli was robbed by wicked fate. He finished the first edition almost 37 minutes ahead of Ganna in terms of total elapsed time, and in 1911 he was 34 minutes clear of Galetti. Never let it be said that bike racing used to be fair.

In 1911, politics intervened when Italy went to war. Giuseppe Garibaldi and the nation's other Patres Patriae were united by a belief in self-determination and Italian nationalism, but the Red Shirts were always more of a revolutionary guard than an imperial army. There were others, however, who once in power would embrace the idea of empire quite zealously, and, by the turn of the twentieth century, and largely under the influence of the bellicose two-time prime minister Francesco Crispi (the Sicilian once compared himself to Mount Etna in a speech to the Italian parliament), the still juvenile nation had set itself on a course to war. Crispi had been a friend and confidant of Garibaldi and even more radical republicans like Giuseppe Mazzini, but over time he abandoned most of his liberal ideals in favour of national expansion and centralised control. For this reason, and several others, many see Crispi as the precursor to Benito Mussolini a few decades later.

War – and empire building – was seen as a viable method by which to create nationalist sentiment among the country's mostly isolated and uninterested population. Upon its inception, Italy, according to the English historian Denis Mack Smith, had a ground army boasting more troops on the peninsula than Britain had deployed across its vast empire, some 400,000 souls, and by the turn of the century the government spent more on its enormous navy than it did on education, sanitation and public works combined. What it did not have were enemies. The continent's principle powers all considered their southern neighbour to be a bit of a nuisance and an embarrassing ally but other than that they gave Italy little or no thought. Despite its size and its funding, the Italian military had proven itself to be a poor fight force very early on in its career – the 1866 Battle of Lissa saw the vastly outnumbered Austrian Empire defeat the Italians in the Adriatic, off the coast of modern-day Croatia – and the country was never genuinely considered a credible colonial power by its peers. As the German statesman Otto von Bismarck sardonically put it, Italy had a great appetite, but very poor teeth. It was a hunger that had to be satiated, however, and with tensions high across Europe, Italy decided to test its mettle in the area by invading Ottoman-controlled Libya on 29 September 1911. In isolation, the Tripolitanian War was of little consequence, but in the larger European context it proved to be a decisive moment in the continent's lurch to conflict. Technology played a huge part – the Genovese pilot Giulio Gavotti had the dubious honour of being the first man to use an aerial bomb in anger – and the world was given a frightening glimpse of the horrors of modern warfare, but the campaign also proved significant because, encouraged by the relatively easy manner in which the Italians defeated the Turks, nationalists in the Balkans set into motion events that would eventually lead to the assassination of Archduke Franz Ferdinand of Austria in Sarajevo and the outbreak of the First World War.

Sensing an appetite for patriotism, and perhaps with a mind to endear himself to those in power, Cougnet, now the sole owner of the *Gazzetta dello Sport*, decided to try something that could potentially add some loyalist lustre to his marquee event. The Bersaglieri are an eccentricity of the Italian military, famous for their wide-brimmed hats, decorated with the long black plumage of the capercaillie bird, and for the distinctive way in which they march, at a rapid trot, to trumpeters. It is a high-mobility unit, and as such, at the outbreak of war, many cyclists found themselves conscripted. Cougnet's idea was to allow regiments to compete in the 1912 Giro as teams of four riders, with the results of the best three riders on each squad accounting for the final overall classification, which would be awarded to the best group rather than individual. It was, in theory, an interesting idea, but it had to be quickly abandoned when almost anyone serving in the army who could ride a bicycle proffered a palmarès that would have given the likes of Ganna and Galetti pause for thought. The Giro might have been tough in those days, but it was better than an African trench. Relativity is a wonderful thing.

In the end, the race organisation settled for one symbolic team from the Bersaglieri, led by a young Carlo Oriani, with the rest of the squads made up of trade teams under the banners of the various bike manufacturers. Riding for Atala-Dunlop, Carlo Galetti set about defending his title alongside Giovanni Micheletto, and his friends and sometimes rivals, Eberardo Pavesi and Luigi Ganna. It was to be a short Giro – 2,443 kilometres over nine stages, starting in Milan and finishing in Bergamo and going no further south than Rome – and one with a small peloton. Of the 56 riders who started, just 26 finished. Atala won comfortably, with three stage wins, and had it been run as an individual event, the title would have been Galetti's. It was not an experiment that the *Gazzetta* ever chose to repeat.

Oriani and the rest of the Italian army were demobilised by the end of the summer, and the 23-year-old returned quickly to Milan and to his bicycle. Born in a suburb north of Milan on the road to Monza, he was a bricklayer by trade, but also a committed and talented racer, with the kind of squat build and brawny legs that wouldn't look out of place in a modern sprint. In fact, just a week after returning to the Bel Paese, it was with a sprint that he proved just how good he was, beating allcomers to win the Giro di Lombardia in a thrilling finish. Having come fifth in the inaugural Giro, but, crucially, first in the category for independent riders who raced without a team, he was now ready to have a proper go at Italy's most prestigious event.

The 1913 Giro featured a peloton made up exclusively of Italians, and began with a 341-kilometre slog from Milan to Genoa, which was won by the Piemontese Giuseppe Santhià. He was still leading after stage four, the race having worked itself down south, when he lost the lead to Eberardo Pavesi on a horrific stage to Bari that was marred by terrible road conditions and ended up taking some riders as long as 20 hours. The next day's stage finished in Campobasso, a hilltop town in the Molise region that would become an important fixture in the Giro's future sojourns down south, and was won by a young Costante Girardengo, a name to remember. Pavesi retained the GC lead, but Oriani, yet to win a stage but never far from the action, was sitting pretty in second. Stage seven spelled disaster for Pavesi, the victim of a crash, who dropped out of the running for general classification after finishing 18th, relinquishing the lead temporarily to Giuseppe Azzini who would, the next day, pass it on to Oriani. Azzini made the blunder of all blunders on stage eight, stopping to get some food in a restaurant only to fall asleep after his meal from pure exhaustion, but Oriani's win was probably more the result of some astute tactical thinking on his part. He'd been consistently good without ever needing to be brilliant, and as the modern era of racing has proven time and again, that's the surest strategy for anyone looking for glory. He was the first rider to ever win a grand tour without taking a stage victory.

The bricklayer was a popular champion. Known for his gregarious personality and a very healthy appetite – his nickname was 'El Pucia', a phrase in dialect relating to the way in which he'd mop up every last bit of sauce from his plate with a piece of bread – reports of the day recall Oriani's screaming fans in Milan singing, 'Che crepa la vacca, ma che 'riva el Pucia', a phrase in the local dialect that somewhat defies translation but means roughly, 'Let the cow die, as long as el Pucia wins.' Strong stuff coming from a gang of farmers. He retired from the race the following year midway through and would never get the chance to race again. El Pucia rejoined the Bersaglieri at the outbreak of war later in 1914, serving bravely on the front with Austria for three years, when tragedy struck.

Caught in the middle of an assault by the Habsburg troops

during the Battle of Caporetto, Oriani narrowly avoided capture by using his rudimentary Bersaglieri bicycle to retreat. During his escape, the young soldier discovered one of his compatriots drowning in the icy waters of the Tagliamento river and quickly dived in to save him. In doing so, he sealed his own fate. Still 12 years before the discovery of penicillin, the basic medicine of the day was incapable of saving the winner of the fifth Giro d'Italia from pneumonia. In an attempt to see if a warmer climate might save him, he was transferred to a hospital in Caserta, just north of Naples, but it was no use. On 3 December 1917, Oriani died, with his young wife by his bedside, a month after his 29th birthday.

SALITA FAMOSA

ROCCARASO, ABRUZZO

The first mountain to ever take the Giro d'Italia above 1,000 metres, Roccaraso is not going to trouble a twenty-first-century racer. It was the final climb of the 2016 Giro's sixth stage and the young Belgian Tim Wellens made it look easy, striking out solo from a breakaway, attacking the other riders in a group of six escapees on the lower slopes to ride alone all the way to the finish as the general classification contenders scrambled for position.

It was, however, a very different proposition back in 1909. The inaugural race passed through the town from the east, midway through a 243-kilometre, coast-to-coast stage from Chieti to Naples. That maiden peloton tackled it while perched on saddles made from thick leather and riding sluggish frames of straight-gauge steel, with only one gear to turn their wheels, which were heavy combinations of stout tyres glued with shellac to wooden rims.

Riders preferred a fixed gear whenever possible, but as the race went higher and descending became a vital skill, freewheels quickly became common on hillier stages to avoid having to remove one's feet from the pedals on the faster downhill sections. The lucky few could count on double-sided hubs, which allowed them to stop and change their set-up at key moments in the race. Gear ratios were low compared to modern standards, but the riders were used to spinning, which is probably a remnant of the sport's roots on the track, where higher cadences are normal. The brakes of the day provided more slowing power than stopping power, and were generally a mix of crude top pads that pressed down on the tyre and early versions of the now-ubiquitous caliper system.

With a pump for the inevitable flats and a handlebar bag for food, the best racing bike that money could buy weighed almost as much as three of today's machines, and because the roads were unpaved and often treacherously boggy, the wheelbase was much longer to allow for a more relaxed geometry that could cope with the rigours of the road surface while still being able to handle predictably. At Roccaraso, heavy rain could cut gorges through the sandy foundations and leave the surface uneven, erratic and pockmarked with potholes, and in places the top covering of gravel often looked less like a mixture of pebbles and grit, and more like a loosely packed ribbon of tyre-shredding shale, twisting its way up through forest and the medieval villages that still cling to hilltops deep in the Apennines. Suffice to say that Luigi Ganna and Carlo Galetti had their work cut out for them.

More recently, Roccaraso was the scene of a famous victory by Fausto Coppi, who was first across the line in the fourth stage of the 1953 Giro d'Italia. Earlier that day, Hugo Koblet crashed into a young girl, who was cheering on the passing peloton and throwing flowers, perilously close to the roadside. The Swiss legend shot out of the preceding bend at breakneck speed, desperately trying to keep touch with an attack, when the child jumped out unexpectedly to collect a souvenir discarded by another rider. It happened too quickly for the fast-moving Koblet to avoid, and so he slammed right into her, suffering a heavy blow as he landed. The girl was miraculously unharmed, but Koblet was unconscious for some time, and had to be revived by his teammates who found him in the dirt, badly cut and with his bike destroyed from the collision. With their leader resuscitated and on a new bike, the Swiss dug deep to catch the main pack, which had elected to slow down in a somewhat unusual display of virtue. Once back at the front, the bandaged Koblet was part of an illustrious group – including Gino Bartali, Fiorenzo Magni, and Louison Bobet – to be beaten by the matchless Coppi in a bunch sprint.

It's a climb that Giro organisers tend to use sparingly, and before 2016 it had been 29 years since the race's last visit, when the punchy classics specialist Moreno Argentin took glory. The modern route is 17 kilometres long, with an average 4.8 per cent gradient that peaks at 12 per cent in its opening stretch. It features a little false-flat drag around the midway point, before picking up again and finishing with a final run at 7 per cent.

These days, Roccaraso is more famous as one of central Italy's main ski resorts, offering city dwellers some snowy escapism less than two hours from Rome and Naples, but it holds a special place in the hearts of the Giro's *appassionati*.

3

ALFREDO BINDA: IL GRANDE ANTIPATICO

Before Coppi, before Bartali, there was Binda. Costante Girardengo might have been Italy's first *Campionissimo*, the champion of champions, but Binda was cycling's first cannibal, decades before the Belgian Eddy Merckx would earn that famous sobriquet by ravaging every race and rider that he came up against. Binda was a rider of unparalleled ability, of such unique talent that he dominated almost every race he entered. In 14 years as a professional, he won the Giro five times, four Italian national titles, four editions of the Giro di Lombardia, three World Championships, two Milano–Sanremo titles and a plethora of other events, including two stages of the Tour de France, in the year that the *Gazzetta dello Sport* paid him not to ride the Giro. His record of 41 stage wins stood for 70 years, until Mario Cipollini went one better in 2003. Binda's rule was not a benign hegemony. His dominance became so overbearing that his detractors called him Il *Dittatore*, the Dictator. Carlo Bergoglio, a journalist for the Turin-based magazine, *Guerin Sportivo*, was an admirer but jokingly dubbed him 'Il *Grande Antipatico*', an epithet that could be loosely translated as 'The Great Unlikeable'.

To his rivals, his presence made their failure an almost foregone conclusion. To the fans, that made the racing boring, which meant that to organisers, Binda's virtuosity was also an inherent vice. His mere appearance at the start threatened to damage, even destroy, the race. And so they paid him to stay home.

Born in August 1902 in Cittiglio, just above Lake Maggiore in the province of Varese, about 60 kilometres northwest of Milan, he emigrated as a teenager in order to ease the burden on his parents (he was the tenth of 14 children), going to live with an uncle in Nice, where he began riding in his spare time while apprenticed as a plasterer. But when he took up racing in the autumn of 1921, it was immediately clear that Binda was special. He was the complete package: powerful on the flats, imperious in the mountains, said to be blessed with a seemingly effortless pedal stroke and an easy elegance under pressure. The French rider René Vietto famously remarked that if Binda started the race with a glass of milk on his back, it would still be full at the finish-line. Renowned as a snappy dresser, and something of a ladies man, the grace that Binda displayed on the bike was said to have been mirrored by a gentlemanly demeanour when off it. But not all aspects of his lifestyle were quite so refined. For one, he was famous for being quite lazy when he wasn't racing, often sleeping until noon, something that would have seemed absurd to Italy's peasantry and proletariat, used as they were to toiling from sun-up to sundown. He was also a regular smoker, and said to sometimes fill his bidons with more than just water.

You might think that a rider like that would be hugely popular, but the Italian public were slow to take to Binda. He was too good for his own good. He'd started winning as soon as he turned professional, and by the time he was 20 he was regularly beating the best riders from both France and Italy. As just one example of how dominant he was in his pomp, cycling lore has it that 'Il Trombettiere di Cittiglio' – another of his nicknames, for he was an accomplished trumpeter in his spare time – was able to shower and take the train home to Varese before the last rider crossed the finish line of the 1926 Giro di Lombardia, a race he won from second-placed Antonio Negrini by almost 30 minutes. Cycling has always thrived on rivalry – there's little point in a race if you know the outcome at the start, after all – and from the second he made his debut for the legendary Legnano team until his retirement almost a decade and a half later, Binda lacked a consistent challenger. His first Giro came in 1925, when the first Campionissimo, Costante Girardengo, was already in decline, and though Learco Guerra occasionally got one over on him, the latter's only Giro title came in 1934, the year a 32-year-old Binda retired midway through.

From the beginning, it was clear that Binda was bad for business. Appearing in the famous green jersey of the Legnano team, the little-known Binda would make an immediate and lasting impression on the Italian public in the 1925 Giro. The 13th edition, some 3,520 kilometres spread out over 12 stages, was supposed to be a straight battle between Legnano's Giovanni Brunero and Girardengo, riding for Wolsit alongside Gaetano Belloni. Between them, that trio had won five of the last six Giri. One of them would probably have taken the 1924 edition, too, had it not been for the fact that none of them had taken part. The sport's biggest names were beginning to get a sense of their own worth by that time, and so demanded that their teams pay them to take part, regardless of results. The teams, in turn, called for the race organisation to foot the bill, and a standoff ensued that allowed Giuseppe Enrici, an American-born Italian citizen, to win the biggest race of his career against a weak peloton of journeymen and chancers, lured onto their bicycles by the Gazzetta's panicked promise of room and board for the duration of the race.

Pietro Linari, a teammate of Brunero and Binda, took the honours on 1925's first stage, after 278 kilometres of racing from Milan to Turin, but all of the major favourites finished right behind him. Stage two headed towards the coast in Liguria, finishing in Arenzano, 30 kilometres west of Genoa along the Costa Azzurra. The win went to Girardengo, but both Brunero and Binda, his young *gregario* (the Italian term for a support rider within a team), finished on the same time, with the Trombettiere ahead of his leader in the classification. The 315 kilometres to Pisa on stage three cost Brunero more than four minutes, but they couldn't separate Girardengo and his young rival, Binda, who both finished on the same time as the day's winner, Girardengo's teammate, Pierino Bestetti. The following stage was almost 14 hours long, but still they were neck and neck, and after more than 1,200 kilometres and 45 hours of racing, the duo began stage five to Naples joint top of the general classification.

As the race headed south, the plot thickened. Rumour had it that Gaetano Belloni was a little upset with his friend Girardengo. The Campionissimo had worked hard to help earn Bestetti the win with little regard to Belloni's travails. He'd lost 16 minutes that day to bad form or bad fortune, and at least part of the blame, as far as Belloni was concerned, lay with his colleagues from Wolsit. For a rider of his stature – he'd already won the Giro in 1920, Milano–Sanremo twice and two of an eventual three titles at the Giro di Lombardia – this was a slight that couldn't be ignored. And so, when the opportunity presented itself, Belloni took his revenge, working with Binda to attack Girardengo when he flatted on the way from Rome to Naples. Belloni's treachery was rewarded with the stage win, but it was his 22-year-old accomplice who profited most, finishing the day with a lead of five-and-a-half minutes over Girardengo, whose hopes of a third Giro title had been dealt a deadly blow.

The gap would not have seemed fatal at the time – Enrici had won by almost an hour the year before – but for the rest of the Giro, the crowd favourite Girardengo just couldn't shake Binda from his wheel. He bounced back from his disaster in Naples with a win two stages later in Benevento, but the race leader rolled in just 28 seconds behind. Brunero won stage eight to Sulmona, but Girardengo and Binda were just behind him, the hitherto king of Italian roads stalked mercilessly by his fresh-faced heir apparent. The next three stage victories went to the Campionissimo, but Binda never failed to finish immediately after, refusing to cede so much as a second, and by the time the peloton rolled out of Verona on stage 12, bound for Milan, there must have been an air of deflated resignation to the Wolsit team, even as Belloni took the final stage win. Their superstar, nine times the Italian national champion, twice the Giro d'Italia winner and the dominant force at races the length and breadth of the peninsula for more than half a decade, had been bested by a kid. Little did they know that the kid was just getting started.

The following year, a bad crash on the first stage put Binda out of contention for the general classification, but he laboured on in the service of Brunero, who would become the first man to officially win the event three times, Carlo Galetti having succeeded twice under his own name in 1910 and 1911, and again the following year, when the race was run as a team event. After initially wanting to retire, the defending champion ignored the fact that he was 40 minutes down on the leaders and set about proving himself to be the strongest rider in the field, winning six stages, guiding his teammate to the title and eventually finishing second, 15 minutes adrift of Brunero but an impressive 40 minutes ahead of the third-placed Arturo Bresciani. Costante Girardengo, having lead until stage six, retired the following day with an injury. Time was catching up with the Campionissimo, and while he'd race on with some success for another nine years, the man who had once been the pride of a nation would never win another stage at the Giro d'Italia.

Binda's victory the following year was, in a word, vicious. The race covered 15 stages and more than 3,758 kilometres, and while 258 riders started in Milan, only one of them mattered. The 24-year-old led the general classification from day one and triumphed in all but three stages, and while the organisers had decided to introduce a time bonus of a minute for every stage victory, they didn't really matter, because even without them he'd have finished more than a quarter of an hour ahead of his fellow Legnano rider, Brunero. It was a tyrannical display of superiority, and the perfect illustration of why champions need challengers. He won sprints and he won in the mountains. Only once did he surrender time on the three stages that he didn't win, when he gave up a minute and 50 seconds to Arturo Bresciani on the 215-kilometre route from Pescara to Pesaro on stage 11. The baying crowds in Rome had seen him cross the line more than eight minutes ahead of Brunero, and the following day in Naples he entertained the tifosi right after winning the sprint by grabbing a trumpet and joining a band on the roadside, just to prove how little the victory had affected him. He'd top off the season by winning the UCI's inaugural World Championships at the Nürburgring in Germany, beating the runner-up Girardengo by seven minutes.

The 16th Giro d'Italia wasn't quite so despotic, but it wasn't far off, and perhaps the most interesting thing that one could say about it was that, at 298, it holds the record for the largest ever number of starters. Domenico Piemontesi, who'd won bronze in Germany behind Binda and Girardengo, took control of the race early and managed five stage wins, but never regained control of the general classification after haemor-rhaging more than 13 minutes to Binda on stage four. After 12 stages and 3,044 kilometres of racing, the Trumpeter fin-ished 18 minutes and 13 seconds ahead of Giuseppe Pancera two weeks later in Milan, having mopped up five stage victories along the way. His younger brother Albino won the other. He played trombone.

By 1929, race fans were fed up. The 17th edition featured a smaller field, just 166, of more talented riders and had a relatively short average length of 209 kilometres for its 14 stages, but the changes mattered not a jot. There were no time bonuses, but Binda finished almost four minutes ahead of Domenico Piemontesi in the general classification and set a record for eight successive stage victories that has never been bettered. It would actually have been nine, had the judges not disqualified the first four across the line on stage 13, after a messy sprint was deemed to be in violation of the rules. Taking to the podium in the Arena Civica, a neoclassical stadium at the centre of Milan's Parco Sempione, Binda was booed for his brilliance. There was no doubt that he was what the Italians call *Fuoriclasse*, beyond classification, but after Giro victory number four, the public was largely beyond caring.

What happened next is improbably shady, even by the grubby standards of professional cycling. In a desperate bid to liven things up, Armando Cougnet and the rest of the race's organisers had an idea. They had to convince Binda to stay at home.

Nowadays, it's rarely confirmed but generally accepted as commonplace that race organisers will offer the sport's biggest names undisclosed appearance fees to take to the start-line. Events like the one-day Classics, the Tour, and the Giro are their own draw, but for smaller stage races and one-day competi-tions, a household name or two can be the distinction between failure and success. And so palms are crossed with silver. In 1930, Binda was bribed to do the opposite. They wanted him as far away from the action as possible. The *Gazzetta dello Sport* paid him the equivalent of the winner's purse to skip the Giro and try his hand at the Tour de France. That means that he earned 22,500 lire without so much as pinning on a race number or turning a crank, and given professional cycling's proudly avaricious nature, that coup must surely rank as the greatest success in the history of the sport.

In Binda's absence, 115 riders took to the start with the best chance they'd had in years of actually winning something. For the first time in the event's history, it started in the south – way south – in Messina, on the island of Sicily, where it spent three days before returning to the mainland. It was a year of firsts at the Giro, because an up-and-coming star by the name of Learco Guerra won the first of his career's 31 stages while Luigi Marchisio became the race's youngest ever GC champion, just a month after his 21st birthday. Unfortunately, that triumph was to prove the zenith of Marchisio's career, but the organisers and the fans weren't to know that. Along with Guerra and Luigi Giacobbe, who finished second aged 23, the future of the competition looked bright. Binda's dominance might not be so absolute in future.

After failing as a footballer, Guerra turned to cycling relatively late in life, turning professional in 1928. By the 1930 Giro, he was 28 and already recognised as one of the country's most talented cyclists, and though he never really became the 'anti-Binda' that so many race fans dreamed of, he was one of the few who could hold a candle to Cittiglio's Campionissimo. He joined Binda that summer in France as part of a star-studded Italian national team and enjoyed a better race than his captain, finishing second to the French favourite André Leducq and winning three stages. He even held the Maillot Jaune for a week.

Binda, for his part, failed to live up to his billing but nevertheless went home a very happy man. Such was his fame that he'd convinced Henri Desgrange, the Tour's founder, to break one of his cardinal rules. He paid Binda a start fee. With his teammate Guerra in yellow, the four-time Giro champion was sitting comfortably in third when he crashed on the seventh stage, losing an hour to his rivals in the general classification. Three days later, he abandoned the race in the Pyrenees. At the time, his departure puzzled both his opponents and the press, because despite the accident he'd bounced back in typically vigorous fashion by winning the following two stages. Years later, he would reveal that the real reason he'd returned to Italy was that the *Gazzetta* hadn't paid up and he was getting worried about the welfare of his non-appearance fee. Retiring from that Tour was, he admitted, the one great regret in a lifetime of satisfactions.

Both 1931 and 1932 were disappointments for the erstwhile unbeatable Trombettiere. Resplendent in the rainbow stripes of the World Champion's jersey, Binda was welcomed back to the 19th edition of the Giro and started in scintillating form, winning twice and leading the general classification until a bad crash in the capital on stage six forced him to retire with a back injury. Though he was not without his supporters, Binda's departure delighted many of the more colourful tifosi, who had been whipped into a rage several days previously when Cougnet took an executive decision to award a tight sprint finish between Guerra and Binda to the latter. Photo evidence would later prove the director right, but when it was posted for all to see in a shop window in downtown Pescara, where the stage had finished, the offending storefront was duly vandalised and the picture torn to shreds. In some ways, it's comforting to know that the refusal of the sport's partisan fans to let evidence get in the way of a resentful frenzy isn't a modern manifestation.

The following year, Binda struggled for form all spring and while he started the 20th Giro as Legnano's captain, he graciously slipped into a supporting role for Antonio Pesenti when Pesenti savaged the peloton with an explosive attack on the seventh stage. The pair were technically on different teams, but with the same man writing the cheques, so Binda was able to help Pesenti hold on to the pink jersey until the finish and go home relatively satisfied with an uninspiring, but professional, performance. And before anyone could write the season off as a disaster, he headed south to Rome for the World Championships, where he comfortably beat his compatriot Remo Bertoni to take his third rainbow jersey. It's a record matched only by Spain's Óscar Freire and the Belgians Rik Van Steenbergen and Eddy Merckx.

Binda was back at the Giro with his rainbow jersey in 1933 for his swansong. The 21st edition was arguably the first 'modern' Corsa Rosa, with 17 stages averaging a humane 197 kilometres each. It was also the first time that the race featured an individual time trial, and a specific prize for the best climber, the Gran Premio della Montagna, these days commonly abbreviated to GPM. No prizes for guessing who benefited the most from these innovations: Binda was more than a minute faster than second-placed Joseph Demuysère in the TT and the first to all four of the GPM summits. By this stage, the Giro was attracting a stellar crowd of foreign racers, but the main duel was between the ageing Binda and the hungry, more popular Guerra. The two were neck and neck, trading blows like prize-fighters, until the boxing analogy came a little too close to reality on stage six in Rome. Racing for the line, the duo were battling for position when Guerra crashed trying to overtake his rival. Guerra was furious, but the jury ruled that it had been a tree, and not his adversary's arm, that caused the fall. In almost the exact same spot where Binda's 1931 Giro had come undone, Guerra's quest for the 1932 Maglia Rosa ended. Binda, without his only genuine antagonist to interrupt him, was free to solo to a record fifth title, winning five of the remaining stages and the last of his career on the finale to Milan. Decades later, the brilliant journalist Gianni Brera, whose name now officially adorns the same stadium in downtown Milan where boos once rang out for Binda, wrote of the great champion: 'For me, Alfredo was the greatest product of Italian cycling. Even though I have the soul of a Coppi fan, I must make room for rationale.' But he hadn't finished yet. Like any self-respecting musician, the Trumpeter would be back in the limelight for an encore, reinventing himself as a conductor to a new band of prodigiously talented performers. Some of his best work was still to come.

4

THE DEVIL WEARS WOOL SHORTS

The 1924 Giro d'Italia could easily have been a dud. With all of Italy's best riders striking in protest over payment, there were no big-name draws and the peloton was made up of relative unknowns, riding for themselves as independents and supported only by the race organisation. But having staved off disaster and proven a point to the protesting teams by promising provisions to the race's field of 90 freelancers, Armando Cougnet, Emilio Colombo, and the 12th edition of the Corsa Rosa received a massive publicity boost from the unlikeliest of sources.

According to contemporary reports, the organisers stocked up before the first stage, buying almost 5,000 bananas, thousands of bottles of water, more than 700 eggs, 600 chickens, three quarters of a tonne of raw meat and a host of other groceries. One thing that wasn't on the shopping list was a rider with two X chromosomes, but a female athlete was about to grab the headlines, in equal measure both titillating and scandalising Italy's patriarchal society, some 21 years before women would even get the vote.

Castelfranco Emilia is a small town on the road between Bologna and Modena, famous for being the birthplace of tortellini, delicious ring-shaped parcels of egg pasta traditionally stuffed with meat or cheese. It is less well known for being the home town of the only woman to ever ride a grand tour, but it was there that Alfonsa Rosa Maria was born in the spring of 1891 to Carlo Morini and Virginia Marchesini, a peasant couple. The second of four daughters and six sons in the Morini household, young Alfonsina – '-ina' is a common diminutive in Italian – was a tomboy, learning to ride at an early age on the bicycle that her father used as transportation to and from the fields. She was impressively fit and full of energy, in a period when typhoid, tuberculosis and malnutrition were a constant threat to Italy's underclasses. It was unusual to allow a girl to behave in an overtly masculine way – the locals in Castelfranco Emilia were said to refer to her as 'the Devil in the dress' as she flew about on her bicycle with no attention paid to conventional etiquette – but her parents don't seem to have been too bothered by propriety. After all, Alfonsina's older sister Emma had been born out of wedlock, an event that must have created some scandal among the local community of deeply religious peasants. And the Morinis weren't afraid of work, either, because as well as their own offspring, they regularly took in children from the local orphanage in return for payment.

But unconventional as they might have been, Alfonsina's parents weren't overly enamoured when they found out that she'd begun racing rather than attending mass or dedicating herself to becoming a seamstress. There was pressure on her to quit, but at 14 she married Luigi Strada, a local mechanic and engraver, who quickly moved her to Milan and, as a wedding gift, bought her the best bicycle he could afford. He was by all accounts a modern-minded, intelligent man, who saw his new wife's passion for cycling as not only natural and healthy, but also a great opportunity. In one fell swoop, Alfonsina had found a husband, a fan, a manager, and an escape from the crippling monotony of peasant life in Emilia-Romagna. It was to be a happy partnership for many years and Luigi proved to be a capable agent and fountain of constant support, before eventually meeting a miserable end in 1942, when he died in an asylum for the mentally disturbed.

Some versions of the Strada story have it that she lined up at the 1924 Giro incognito, cropping her hair and signing on as the more ambiguous-sounding 'Alfonsin'. In truth, while her short and stocky build was indisputably boyish and her unruly curls were generally kept short, she was still very obviously feminine. On top of that, by the mid-1920s any intentional deception would have been difficult to pull off, because she was by then something of a star. By the end of the twentieth-century's first decade, Alfonsina had established herself as the leading female cyclist, and was even given a special medal by Tsar Nicholas II at the Grand Prix of St Petersburg in 1909. She also set a new Hour Record for women in Turin in 1911, posting an impressive 37.192 kilometres on the Moncalieri track. For context, Lucien Petit-Breton set a record of 41.1 kilometres just a few years before, in Paris. And according to the Italian sports historian Paolo Facchinetti, Strada enjoyed several years of both celebrity and success in the French capital, after a correspondent from the *Gazzetta* recommended her to a group of entrepreneurs looking to add novelty and excitement to their track events. That loose connection with the Giro's organisers would be enough to question any suggestions of subterfuge in 1924, but there's more evidence that Cougnet and Colombo knew exactly who she was when she lined up in Milan. She had, after all, competed officially in the 1917 edition of the Giro di Lombardia, after Cougnet himself had decided that there was technically no rule forbidding the entrance of female competitors.

She finished that day dead last, an hour and a half behind the winner, the Belgian Philippe Thys. But she did finish, which is more than could be said for some 20 sorry souls who'd had to abandon because of mechanicals, crashes or sheer exhaustion. It was a performance that won her the admiration and friendship of a young Costante Girardengo, among others.

Strada's presence in the 1924 Giro peloton must have been the subject of some debate between Colombo and Cougnet. There was the danger that the scandal of it would have a negative impact, or that the gimmicky inclusion of a woman might devalue the race's reputation as a sporting contest. Ultimately, though, Colombo was in the business of selling newspapers, and there was no doubt that Alfonsina's exploits were of interest to readers. La Regina della Pedivella, the Queen of the Cranks, as her fans called her, was allowed to stick around. For her part, Alfonsina wanted to do more than make up the numbers or shift a few copies of the Gazzetta. She was there to show what she could do, and her campaign started well. Strada lost time to the leaders on the opening 300-kilometre slog from Milan to Genoa, but finished respectably in the middle of the pack. Likewise, on the following stages to Florence, Rome and then Naples, she consistently arrived a couple of hours behind those battling for the general classification, but invariably ahead of many of her less gifted male counterparts. Things came undone for her on the eighth stage from L'Aquila to Perugia, when a series of flats and falls left her painfully wounded and well outside of the organisation's cut-off time. Given that she'd made it to Perugia at all – one report claims that she used a broomstick to mend her broken handlebars after one particularly bad crash – there were some among the race jury that wanted to extend a courtesy to the Giro's only female contestant and allow her to continue. In the end, however, the dissenters won out and Strada was officially disqualified. Unofficially, there was a small victory. Given the courage she'd displayed, and no doubt with an eye on newspaper revenue, Colombo offered to foot the bill personally for her room and board so that she might continue. She would be allowed to persevere to the finish in Milan, but would not be counted on the GC. The rules had been bent to find a solution agreeable to everyone's interests. This is Italy, after all.

While Pittsburgh's own Giuseppe Enrici tightened his stranglehold on the race, which he went on to win, the 34-year-old Strada entertained the crowds all the way to the end, stopping for autographs and handing out photographs along the route, before finishing the 3,613 kilometres more than 38 hours behind the winner. It was almost twice as far behind as the last recognised finisher, however, and once the heavy hitters like Girardengo returned the following year, there was no desire on the organisation's part to let her have another go. The gamble, however, had paid off for everyone involved. It filled ream after ream of newsprint for Colombo and for Alfonsina, and her heroics that year would later inspire popular stories and books that reached far beyond the boundaries of the cycling world. Strada used the fame to full effect, building a career from it and competing across both Italy and France for decades afterwards. In later life, she remained a constant on the Italian cycling scene, regularly attending races and entertaining the likes of Fausto Coppi whenever the great and the good passed through Milan. She died aged 68, of a heart attack, when her bright red Moto Guzzi 500 fell on top of her outside her home. She'd just returned from cheering on the riders at the 1959 Tre Valli Varesine.

CROCE D'AUNE, VENETO

For the most part, the Passo Croce d'Aune is an unremarkable climb. At least in the context of its surroundings. It barely tips 1,000 metres at the top, and is predominantly submerged in the sort of thick woodland that suffocates a rider and chokes out the best of the views. Those shortcomings could be forgiven if it boasted the kind of vertiginous grades of a climb such as the Muro di Sormano, but aside from a brief section at the beginning, it never hits double figures and averages out at a mere 7.8 per cent over eight and a half kilometres. There's nothing objectively special about the Croce d'Aune, but thanks to a twist of fate almost a century ago, it holds a unique place in cycling lore.

Tullio Campagnolo was born in 1901 to modest circumstances in Vicenza. To the wider world, Vicenza is a small, pretty city most notable for its industrial contribution to the Italian economy and for the works of Andrea Palladio, a sixteenth-century architect whose influence is still prominent half a millennium later, but for cycling fans this little corner of northern Italy has another significance. Tullio's father owned a hardware shop on the Corso Padova, just outside the historical centre of downtown Vicenza, where his son would develop a love of tinkering from an early age. He also developed a love of cycling, and in his spare time Tullio was a competent, if not world-beating, rider.

While competing in the Gran Premio della Vittoria in November 1927, the young Campagnolo stopped on the early slopes of the Croce d'Aune to change his gear – in those days, cyclists had a different cog size on each side of the wheel and changing involved removing and flipping the wheel – only to find that both the bolts, and his hands, were frozen stiff from the cold. Having been in the lead, Tullio saw his advantage disintegrate as he fumbled with the wing nuts. A vow was made to find a solution, and while he lost out on the prize and the podium that day, the spark ignited by his misfortune would fire his imagination, build a business empire and change the face of the sport for ever.

Two and a half years after his spoiled ascent at Croce d'Aune, Campagnolo had a patent for a revolutionary quick-release design and by 1933 his now legendary company had been founded and his quick-release hubs were in production. It's more or less the same system that we use today. And he didn't stop there. In 1940, he invented a dual-rod system dubbed the *Cambio Corsa*, which consisted of two levers and rods attached to the frame's seat stay. One released the rear wheel to allow it to move back and forth in the dropout so that correct chain tension could be maintained, while the lever below guided the chain from one sprocket to the next as the rider back-pedalled. Then, a decade later, the Gran Sport was born, introducing the cable-operated parallelogram rear derailleur system that endures to this day.

Of course, this was a fecund time for technological developments and you could argue that if it hadn't been him, someone else would have stumbled upon these solutions to competitive cycling's most pressing problems sooner or later. But no one person has had a bigger impact on the development of the bicycle or on the sport than Campagnolo, who strived to innovate until his death in 1983. It's impossible to imagine what cycling would look like today without Tullio's influence, which is why the Croce d'Aune deserves a heartfelt *chapeau* for the influence that it had on young Tullio. This humble little climb's effect in the Giro has been minuscule – it was the scene of a chaotic, puncture-riddled descent in 1964 and a wholly uneventful ascent in 2009 – but its effect on the race, on all of cycling, is nothing short of monumental.

5

FASCISM AND THE GIRO

Henri Desgrange began awarding a yellow jersey to the general classification leader of the Tour de France in 1919. It helped fans and journalists to distinguish the overall front-runner, while also serving to subtly reinforce the race's connection to Desgrange's paper, L'Auto, which used yellow newsprint. It wasn't until 1931 that the Gazzetta followed suit, introducing the Maglia Rosa for the 19th edition of the race. And emblazoned on the front was the unmistakable symbol of Benito Mussolini's government: the fasces.

Originating with the Etruscans, the image of the fasces – a bundle of birch rods, tied together to illustrate strength in unity and wrapped around an axe – was an important allegory of state power in ancient Rome. They were carried in a procession before a magistrate to indicate his rank and the power vested in him by the republic. The symbol still features prominently worldwide in government iconography today, not least in the United States, where it has featured on currency and can still be seen behind the podium in the United States House of Representatives, on the official seal of the United States Senate, as part of the Lincoln Memorial, and within a frieze on the facade of the United States Supreme Court building, to name but a few examples. It is, however, most closely associated with Mussolini, who used it as both the emblem and the inspiration for the name of the Partito Nazionale Fascista, the National Fascist Party.

Sport, and in particular one that required superhuman endurance and showcased man's ability to overcoming seemingly impossible odds through courage and hard work, was of great interest to Italy's rulers. Mussolini wasn't a huge fan of the Giro's pink jersey – unsurprisingly, he thought it effeminate – but the usefulness of its appropriation was obvious. Poor health was an endemic problem in early twentieth-century Italy, and among those who had served at the front during the First World War, it was a widely held belief that sickness and infirmity had been the Italian army's most dangerous adversary; indeed, tens of thousands had died away from battle due to illness, not least during the 1918 flu pandemic. The values of strength and perseverance, and the immutable goal of victory, are simple rhetorical tools for any bombastic politician to co-opt, and a nation's dominance in a sporting encounter could easily be extrapolated to prove a point in any discussion of racial supremacy. Mussolini's Fascist regime was arguably the first to see the full political potential of sport, using it not only to glorify the perceived superiority of the Italian race but also in making sport a big part of the country's indoctrination into the party's machismo mentality. It was integral to the cult of Mussolini that his influence be clearly at play in every aspect of Italian society. Or as the 1927 Labour Charter put it: 'The Italian nation is an organism possessing a purpose, a life and means of action superior to those possessed by the individuals, or groups of individuals, of which it is composed. The nation is a moral, political, and economic unity integrally embodied in the Fascist State.' And the state was everywhere. Such was the proliferation of fascist iconography and images of Il Duce, the Leader, that the great novelist Italo Calvino famously remarked that he'd spent the first 20 years of his life with Mussolini's face forever in view.

Calvino wasn't the only one who must have felt this way. The aim of the party was to use omnipresent social influence and control as a means to create what the Fascists called the Nuovo Italiano, the New Italian, a citizen in whom the best of the nation's past and its glorious future at the bleeding edge of culture and technology would be synthesised, and who would replace the traditional representative of the country, the peasant. Fascist Italy harked back to the country's imperial ancient history: the Italians were the descendants of the Romans, and that made Mussolini a twentieth-century Caesar.

To better supervise the development of this new society, the party established several organisations to oversee the population away from school and the workplace. The Opera Nazionale Dopolavoro, loosely translatable as the National Workers' Club, encouraged sporting participation and other party-sanctioned entertainment to the labouring classes, while their children could attend the Opera Nazionale Balilla, named after Giovan Battista Perasso (Balilla was his nickname), a child who, apocryphally, started the 1746 revolt against the Habsburg forces in Genoa by hurling a stone at an Austrian official. Kids as young as six could join the Balilla and learn the ways of the New Italians, and by the 1930s over seven million of them were members, while some four million adults frequented the OND. At a higher level, the Italian Olympic Committee, commonly known as CONI, worked on creating exemplars of sporting brilliance that the party could use for its own ends. When Italy won the 1934 World Cup, which it also hosted, it was Mussolini who distributed the medals to the Azzurri players on the pitch.

And when Primo Carnera knocked out Jack Sharkey in Madison Square Garden in 1933 to become the heavyweight champion of the world, he was quickly enlisted into the Fascist militia before being paraded in full Blackshirt uniform, alongside Il Duce, on his famous balcony in Rome's Piazza Venezia. A massive surge in literacy and the proliferation of broadcasting technology made professional sport an everyday part of people's lives, as they followed it with great interest in the pages of the Gazzetta and on the radio. The party broadcaster, Ente Italiano per le Audizioni Radiofoniche, was founded in 1927, followed by a heavily subsidised rural agency that allowed the broadcaster – and the Fascists' propaganda – to penetrate deep into the previously isolated rural hinterland. With advances in technology, the radio went from being a rare luxury to a common part of daily life. And in spite of the fact that the machine itself still cost more than a month's wage for the average worker, the number of radio subscribers exploded, going from 27,000 in 1926 to over a million by the outbreak of war, with millions more listening regularly to races and matches in clubs, cafés and other public venues.

The Giro wasn't the first cycling-related propaganda tool that the Fascists seized upon. That dubious honour went to Enrico Toti, a tragicomic figure from Rome who lost his leg while working on the railway. Thereafter, Toti used a bicycle to move around and completed several international journeys on two wheels before enlisting – and dying – for the Bersaglieri in the First World War. Vociferously patriotic, even before the war, he was said to have died heroically in the Sixth Battle of the Isonzo in 1916, throwing his crutch at the enemy before flinging himself to his fate. It made for a great story, which the Fascists then embellished before erecting statues to their mutilated martyr across Italy, but other, more believable accounts of his death recall a boisterous drunk being shot by a sniper while off duty. The first professional cyclist to attract the full force of Mussolini's attention was to meet a similarly violent end, but not before every last ounce of agitprop had been wrung from his exploits.

Ottavio Bottecchia was the first Italian to win the Tour de France. He was born in 1891 in San Martino di Colle Umberto, a small town in Friuli, about 70 kilometres north of Venice. Bottecchia, whose family were dirt poor, was the second youngest of nine children. He managed just one year of schooling before becoming an apprentice cobbler and eventually settling into life as a bricklayer, from which his fans would later derive his rather unglamorous sobriquet, Il Muratore del Friuli. By the time he became a professional cyclist, Bottecchia had already endured a hard life, as the crippling poverty of his childhood was followed by four years of fighting with the Bersaglieri in the First World War, during which time he contracted malaria, fell foul of a mustard gas attack and was captured by the Austrians twice, escaping both times, something that later earned him a medal for valour. Even at the height of his wealth and fame he wore a tired, hungry expression, with the parched skin and wizened facial features of a much older man, and as rich as he became he never lost the peasant's existential need to accumulate wealth. Speaking in 1923 to the Gazzetta's correspondent at the Tour de France, Fabio Orlandini, he said: 'I don't race for sport, or for the cheers of the crowd or the flowers from the beautiful women, and even less for the glory. I race for the money, to earn as much as I can, and there will never be enough suffering or fatigue to take my mind off this aim. I race for my family, they're poor and I'll do everything possible so that they don't have to live in misery.' Orlandini noted afterwards that on the pronunciation of misery, 'Bottecchia grimaced with disgust, as if that word was about to make him vomit.'

After migrating to France to find work and discovering the

opportunities available to a cyclist of his abilities, he turned pro in 1920, aged 26, riding as an independent until his performance at the 1923 Giro attracted some admiring glances from his adopted homeland. And though he finished three quarters of an hour behind the pugnacious Girardengo, he still managed fifth place, making him the highest ranked rider without a team. That showing brought him to the attention of Henri Pélissier and the dominant Automoto team across the border, and by June he'd been signed up to ride for Pélissier, that year's eventual winner. Not only that, but Bottecchia also won the second stage from Le Havre to Cherbourg, becoming the first Italian to pull on the Maillot Jaune. The following summer he won a bunch sprint on the first stage, again finishing in Le Havre, and held on to the jersey all the way to the end. The Tour win of 1925 wasn't quite so straightforward early on, but he still won four stages and used his superior climbing ability to put the race beyond his rivals once the Grand Boucle reached the Alps. He eventually arrived in Paris with a lead of over 54 minutes on his teammate, Lucien Buysse.

Obviously, once he began winning in France, the authorities at home took note, but there was a problem. Bottecchia, ever mindful of his roots, was a committed socialist and ardent anti-Fascist. After allegedly teaching himself to read with copies of the *Gazzetta dello Sport*, he was regularly seen with anti-fascist pamphlets, and without ever openly criticising Mussolini or his followers, it didn't take a detective to discover which side of the fence he stood on. So when he died mysteriously in June 1927, plenty of people cried foul play. The 32-year-old was found gravely injured on the side of the road, bloodied and apparently beaten, with a broken collarbone and cracked skull, laid out in a vineyard some distance from his bicycle, which was undamaged and neatly propped up by a post near the road. Officially, he suffered heatstroke and crashed, but given the gruesomeness of the Tour's daily grind and indeed the wretchedness of his life before becoming a cyclist, this seems unlikely. Another theory was that he'd been assaulted by an angry farmer who caught him stealing grapes – years later a local smallholder admitted to the crime, claiming to have hit him over the head with a stone – but even ignoring the fact that Bottecchia was more than wealthy enough to buy his own food, common sense suggests that it would be an odd time of year to pinch grapes, a fruit that is normally harvested in autumn. The third explanation is the most Machiavellian and, unsurprisingly for a country enthralled to conspiracy theories, the most popular in Italy. It holds that Bottecchia, unwilling to play the role of poster boy for a regime he despised, was murdered by Mussolini's Blackshirts. There's no evidence to prove this, of course, but there's nothing to disprove it either, and political killings were not uncommon at the time. Whatever the cause, after surviving penury and hunger as a child, bullets and bombs as a young adult, and the perils of the Tour de France as a professional cyclist, Ottavio Bottecchia died 12 days later in hospital, just a month after his brother died in a car crash. As a final insult, the state-run media lauded him as a true expression of the New Italian, while the Blackshirts stood as honour guard for his funeral.

Elsewhere, the government found more acquiescent specimens. The legendary Girardengo, for one, wasn't a demonstrable zealot in his everyday life, but he was often photographed smiling with Fascists and Blackshirts at the races, and was said to be a friend of the Mussolini family. Although that could be down to the fact that the militia was a ubiquitous part of Italian life in the 1920s and 1930s, Girardengo certainly played a part in sports-related propaganda, particularly in his role as national team manager, just before the outbreak of war, when he guided Gino Bartali to his first Tour de France victory. He even went so far as to ostentatiously donate the gates of his villa so that they might be melted down for the nation's benefit. If he was just playing the game, he was doing so very convincingly.

Girardengo's one-time rival, Alfredo Binda, meanwhile, was an unapologetic Fascist, even after the war. That he was unafraid to openly discuss his preference for the losing side might seem surprising – and in the aftermath of the Second World War it was often difficult to find anyone who didn't claim to be an anti-fascist or a partisan – but the fact remains that without the tacit consent of large swathes of the population, it wouldn't have been possible for Mussolini to come to power with his March on Rome in October 1922, let alone hold on to control for two decades afterwards. It's also a common fallacy, outside of Italy, to consider Mussolini's Fascism and the Nazism of Adolf Hitler's Germany as completely analogous. The Fascists had much in common with Hitler and his National Socialist German Workers' Party when it came to political beliefs, rhetoric and bullying tactics, but they did not share the same bloodlust or go to the same extremes. Dissenting voices like Alberto Moravia, who decades later would be elected to the European Parliament representing the Italian Communist Party and still widely celebrated for his anti-fascist novel Il Conformista, exchanged correspondence with senior figures in the party and received state subsidies throughout Mussolini's reign. And while the party eventually developed a propensity towards anti-Semitism, in the twentieth century this was not the preserve of right-wing dictators. In fact, for several years, a Sicilian Jew by the name of Guido Jung served as Mussolini's Minister of Finance, and the journalist Margherita Sarfatti, who came from a wealthy Jewish family in Venice, was a party member who wrote one of the period's most popular and widely distributed biographies of Il Duce. She was also his mistress.

The country's *Leggi razziali*, Race Laws, weren't introduced until the end of 1938, and proved deeply unpopular with several senior party members, including Mussolini's right-hand man, Italo Balbo, who had close ties to the Jewish community in his native Ferrara. The laws were seen not as the realisation of a widely held ambition among the fascist rank and file, but as evidence that Mussolini had become a puppet of Hitler, and they were criticised by the royal family and the Vatican. Elsewhere, there were unquestionably violent crimes committed against fellow Italians, but not so many that it would be impossible for someone to turn a blind eye. The majority of dissenting voices of the time were punished to *confino*, a type of internal exile that banished them to the rural and impoverished corners of the peninsula, something that had been common under the rule of the Bourbon dynasty in southern Italy before unification. There, they were restricted from travelling and forced to report regularly to fascist officials. Carlo Levi, a prominent Jewish artist, writer and anti-Fascist, was one of thousands who were condemned to such punishment in the mid-1930s, and in exile he painted, worked as a medical doctor, and, according to his memoirs, followed the exploits of the Giro d'Italia in the pages of the *Gazzetta*. By modern standards, that kind of sanction seems unthinkable, but it wasn't the Nazi's death camps or Joseph Stalin's gulags. As such, after the Allied liberation of Italy, when the horrors of the conflict became apparent, many held the belief – erroneous though it was – that the Fascists had been more misguided than malicious. Italy never felt the need to contend with the collective guilt, *Kollektivschuld*, that was to shape the German consciousness after the war, and people who had supported the Fascists were not expected to repent in any meaningful way. Later in life, Binda rationalised his consent by pointing out how common it had been, and by saying that as a self-made man of means with traditional,

Catholic beliefs he couldn't very well be a communist. There's an air of blissful ignorance to this defence and indeed, by his own admission, Binda was not a well-educated man – he claimed to have read only one book in his lifetime, Alessandro Manzoni's seminal work I Promessi Sposi (The Betrothed), which is often cited as the most read work of fiction in the Italian language and is, for what it's worth, the favourite novel of the current pope. Perhaps fittingly for a cyclist, it's set in a time of famine and concerns itself primarily with the theme of power – and its ability to inflict suffering on the innocent. Binda never shied from his past loyalties, but insisted that he'd never been much concerned with politics, an assertion that made it easy, years later, for others to airbrush his allegiances from their reverential histories of the man. The fact is, however, that he was political secretary of the local branch of the Fascist Party in his home town of Cittiglio for several years, so he can't have been that disinterested.

Binda's rival, Learco Guerra, was known as a powerful and determined competitor on the bike and a smiling and amiable man off it. Nicknamed La Locomotiva Humana, the Human Locomotive, it was his vigorous sporting ability and forceful riding style that interested the regime, and so they conveniently chose to ignore his cordial personality when building their propagandistic image of him as a superman. As a teenager, Guerra participated in socialist riots in Mantua in early 1920, which ended with six dead civilians after police opened fire on a frenzied crowd. In the subsequent months, he also campaigned on behalf of local left-wing politicians, who swept to a huge majority in council elections. Guerra was said to have been permanently influenced by the Blackshirts' mob mentality and the thuggish violence that would shortly thereafter suppress any opposition to the Fascist party. But regardless of his personal convictions, like everyone else under Mussolini,

Guerra was stuck between a rock and a hard place. So although it was almost certainly done against his wishes, his fame was exploited by the state's propaganda machine and he was promoted as one of their sporting supermen in the late 1920s and 1930s.

In spite of this, he was also wildly popular with the opposition and the country's downtrodden masses. Both he and Binda had come from abject poverty, but unlike his great rival, Guerra never lost his common touch, and his rugged appearance, unrelenting riding style and gregarious demeanour won him legions of fans among Italy's lower classes – particularly in the south. For a regime obsessed by virile masculinity, it's easy to see the attraction of a rider like Guerra. He never quite became a consistent challenge to Binda's supremacy, but he was second to none when it came to feats of preternatural human endurance and, at his best, not even the Campionissimo was a match for his extraordinary tenacity. The perfect illustration of this came in 1931, at the World Championships in Copenhagen. For reasons known only to them, the UCI decided that year to change the road race into a gargantuan time trial, 170 kilometres alone, against the clock, on a pan-flat course. Hammering out an average speed of almost 35 kilometres per hour, the Human Locomotive romped home to victory four minutes and 37 seconds ahead of the runner-up, France's Ferdinand Le Drogo, and more than nine minutes ahead of Binda, the defending champion. Understandably, it was a victory that fostered myths. Some observers claimed that the race had so destroyed Binda that he arrived at the finish-line blind and severely dehydrated. Guerra, untroubled by the hellish, solitary torture that the route promised, was said to have ridden a single-speed bike so as to save on weight. The Gazzetta declared Guerra's performance 'irresistible,' and the Italian railway workers aboard the train that took him home covered the carriages in triumphant graffiti. Similar displays of improbable fortitude came in the Predappio–Roma, also known as the Coppa del Duce, Mussolini's own commemorative race that ran from the dictator's home town, just outside Forlì, to the Italian capital. Like Binda, he won the event twice, his first victory coming in 1930 on a horrific course that was 470 kilometres long and required the peloton to depart from Predappio at nine in the evening and ride through the night, with the roads illuminated by an escort of vehicles, before arriving at the racetrack in the Villa Glori some 18 hours later.

Despite being the first man ever to pull on the Maglia Rosa and winning more Giro d'Italia stages than anyone other than Mario Cipollini and Binda – a total of 31 between 1930 and 1937 – Guerra only triumphed in the general classification once in his career, in 1934. The 22nd edition of the race covered just over 3,700 kilometres in 17 stages, on a course that looked perfect for him because it lacked any really spectacular mountain stages, covered vast distances of rolling countryside, and included two time trials. Binda would retire on the sixth stage following a collision with a motorcycle, turning the race into a two-way battle between the Locomotive and Francesco Camusso, the champion in 1931. It was Camusso who drew first blood, slipping from the leading pack unnoticed just outside Turin to take the opening day's pink jersey. Guerra's response was a masterclass of characteristic belligerence: he took the following two stages from group sprints and then secured the lead in general classification by putting more than two minutes into Camusso on day four's time trial from Livorno to Pisa, covering the 45-kilometre course at a blistering average of over 41 kilometres per hour, a speed that would not look out of place at a professional race today. He followed it with another two stage wins, developing a slender lead of just over a minute ahead of Giuseppe Olmo, who surprised everyone by breaking free of Guerra on stage eight and carving out enough of a gap to grab the jersey, too. But after playing second fiddle to Binda for so many years, Guerra wasn't about to be denied his golden opportunity. As the race returned north the following day from Campobasso in Molise to Teramo in Abruzzo, his rivals were given a proper taste of what the Human Locomotive could do at full steam. By the time Olmo arrived at the finish, he'd lost more than nine minutes and the Maglia Rosa.

Guerra's was the victory that the organisers, the fans, and the Fascists wanted, but it's hard not to feel a little sorry for Camusso, because despite Guerra's 10 stage wins and his superiority against the clock, he only managed to finish 51 seconds ahead of the 1931 champ in second place. To add insult to injury, Guerra had wanted to abandon on stage 13 from Florence to Bologna, when he was left in the dust by Olmo and Camusso at the base of the Passo della Futa, a climb through the Apennines north of Florence that would later be used as part of the Gothic Line, the German Army's last major defence during its retreat from Italy at the end of the Second World War. Rather than allow their star to quit, the Maino team bundled him into the support car and carried on, right in front of the compliant gazes of Cougnet and Colombo, who didn't want to see Guerra leave the race any more than Maino did. He eventually remounted his bicycle and returned to the fray, finishing five minutes behind Olmo, who won a five-man sprint in Bologna. But crucially he remained less than three minutes behind Camusso in the GC, a deficit he'd erase two days later, on stage 14's 50-kilometre time trial to Ferrara, when he finished almost four minutes ahead of the man in pink, who was primarily a climber and never performed well in the TT. With three stages still to go, the race for the pink jersey was over, thanks, at least in part, to a ride in a car. A 32-year-old Guerra finally climbed onto the top step of the Giro's podium on 10 June in Milan, just as Raimundo Orsi and Angelo Schiavio were firing Italy to victory over Czechoslovakia in the World Cup final in Rome's Stadio del Partito Nazionale Fascista, as Mussolini watched from the stands, flanked by King Victor Emmanuel's daughters and Jules Rimet, the FIFA president. It was high tide for Fascist Italy's sporting prestige.

6

BARTALI AND COPPI, COPPI AND BARTALI

It would be impossible to tell the story of the Giro, of cycling, or of Italian sport in general without discussing perhaps its greatest rivalry. Gino Bartali and Fausto Coppi were more than just two of the most exceptional athletes ever to ride a bike: they symbolised, still symbolise, the duality of mid-century Italy and the change that was going on across the country at the time, the old and the new, pre- and post-war, the peasantry of a fading rural identity and the promise of the country's remarkable economic miracle in the 1950s. Bartali stood for the more rural and reserved Old Italy, and Coppi for the modern nation that struggled to find itself in the ashes of Fascism. Bartali, *L'Uomo di Ferro*, the Iron Man. Coppi was crystal, suffering 13 different bone breakages in a career that was all too often interrupted by injury. Bartali was a favourite of the pope and a hero to Italy's persecuted Jews. Coppi, the Campionissimo, Champion of Champions, was more urban and urbane. One often explosive, and always talkative; the other mostly pensive, and always taciturn. Bartali, devout. Coppi, divorced.

Bartali belonged to tradition and to the church. They used

to say that he prayed while he rode and that the saints sometimes offered him favours when the odds were against him.
Coppi, meanwhile, was the living embodiment of post-war
Italy: secular, ambitious, elegant, and effortlessly cool in finely
tailored suits and sunglasses. He believed in himself before
anything else, and had no time to court the favours of guardian
angels.

Almost every aspect of the two men's lives was in stark contrast and the resulting dynamic enchanted a nation and lit up
the cycling world. Bartali worked with the partisans and would
live to the ripe old age of 85, leaving behind Adriana, his wife
of 60 years. Coppi was conscripted into the Italian army and
spent two years as a prisoner of war. There was the scandal of a
failed marriage and an illicit relationship and the tragedy of his
death, a full four decades before his rival, aged just 40. There
were some similarities too, one of them miserable, to which
we'll return in due course.

Gino was born on 18 July 1914 in an unremarkable corner
house on the Via Chiantigiana in Ponte a Ema on the outskirts
of Florence. Fittingly for a boy born on the anniversary of the
Catholic Church's declaration of papal infallibility, his devout
upbringing was profoundly influential. Although there was
something innate about his talent, nurture played a huge part
in his becoming one of the greatest cyclists of all time and one
of the biggest personalities in Italian sport.

Giulia and Torello Bartali were typical of Tuscany's peasant
class at the time. Torello was a bricklayer by trade, while Giulia
worked long hours in the fields before returning home to a side
job embroidering lacework. Legend has it that she gave birth
to Gino just after arriving home from a long journey on foot to
a convent in the countryside to enquire after a housekeeping
position. The Bartalis worked hard for their kids – Gino had
two sisters, Anita and Natalina, and a younger brother, Giulio

– and expected that they would respond in kind. Gino would later recall that he and his brother had helped the women of the house with embroidery work for as long as he could remember, and it was apparently something that the future Giro winner excelled at, but when the boy reached ten, his father felt that it was time for him to find work of his own and so he was sent to earn his keep with some local farmers, collecting the leaves of the raffia palm that once upon a time were used to make ties for grapevines. Nowadays, you're more likely to find it wrapped into the decorative bottoms on cheap, rotund bottles of the local table wine.

It was boring work for a kid with boundless energy, but it was also a means to an end for young Gino. The local school taught only until the age of ten, so he'd need transport to get into Florence and complete his studies. And that meant buying a bicycle, the object of desire for every right-thinking boy the length and breadth of the peninsula. What had started out as an object of torture for the likes of Luigi Ganna and Costante Girardengo, and as a hellish way to put food on the table for the countless other less talented and now forgotten riders of the early Giri, had by the 1920s become a symbol of freedom and speed to *ragazzini* (young Italian boys and girls) everywhere. It would be some time before he'd see a proper racing bike, of course, but the rusty and rudimentary old workhorses of the local labourers had long fascinated the young Gino and when his own arrived, bought with the help of some donations from the family following his first communion, it set in motion a string of events that would change the boy, and bicycle racing, for ever.

He wasn't to know it, but Bartali's future would be inextricably linked to another boy, 300 kilometres to the north. Born five years later than Gino, Angelo Fausto Coppi came into the world on the 15 September 1919, the fourth of five children to Angiolina and Domenico. His parents had moved south to the small town of Castellania from Quarna Sotto, a village not far from Lake Maggiore, to work the land. The family were poor, like so many others, and the children almost certainly malnourished. Fausto grew up thin, with a crooked gait and a gaunt expression that gave no hint of athleticism. Agricultural labour was not for him, and at 13 he found a job in Novi Ligure, the nearest major town, as a delivery boy for a delicatessen. The town happened to be home to Costante Girardengo, the prototype Campionissimo, and, according to legend, his villa was one of young Fausto's stops. Whether there's any truth to the myth or not is of little consequence; while making the rounds with a heavy old bike, laden down with groceries, Coppi fell in love with cycling and found perhaps the only thing in the world to which his gangly, fragile frame was perfectly suited. Standing, his long legs, peculiar posture and barrelled chest looked strange, but in the saddle he was a man transformed into a picture of elegance.

At 15, his uncle and namesake, a sailor, upon returning from sea gave Fausto 520 lire as a gift, and with it he bought a Maino racing bike and began to compete locally and attract attention in the cycling-mad Novi Ligure. Apocryphal encounters with Girardengo aside, one link to the retired champion was formative to Coppi's career: his meeting with Biagio Cavanna, at the time one of Italy's most respected trainers and masseurs. Biagio was a hulk of a man with a big reputation to match. He'd worked with Girardengo and Binda, and by the mid-1930s was looking for the next generation's great hope. Cavanna was famous for his demanding training regimes and later, after going blind, for his dark glasses and the way in which he seemed to see more with his hands than many could with their eyes. The pair formed an immediate and intimate bond, and from that moment until Coppi's death, Cavanna was rarely far from his side.

When Coppi raced as an independent in 1939, the signs were promising. The teenager swept to victory in a host of small, early-season events before making his debut among the professionals at the Giro di Toscana that April. He retired because of a mechanical and most likely went completely unnoticed by the winner and local favourite, Gino Bartali.

Gino's professional career had begun five years earlier, with fireworks. The 1935 Giro was to be the last for the race's first truly great champion, Alfredo Binda, and the debut of a little-known Tuscan, two months shy of his 21st birthday, who would go on to have a profound effect not just on Italian cycling, but on Italian society as a whole.

At the time, the race's seventh day seemed more remarkable for the fact that it was pivotal to Vasco Bergamaschi's overall victory. The 26-year-old Lombard had begun the race in the service of the once formidable Learco Guerra, who was ultimately unable to defend his title from the year before. Bergamaschi up until that point had trailed the Maglia Rosa Giuseppe Olmo – twice winner at Milano–Sanremo but more famous in Italy for his eponymous bicycles – but overturned the lead with an impressive ride to L'Aquila. More impressive still, however, was the performance of the stage winner, the unheralded Bartali, who arrived at the line solo having led for much of the day, putting almost two minutes into his rivals on the Passo delle Capannelle through the Apennines. It was exactly the kind of audacious attack for which Gino would become so famous. In the same season, he made the podium at the Giro di Lombardia and won the Italian national championships. Not content with that, Bartali raced and won in Spain, too.

His Giro triumph in 1936 caused a sensation across the country when he took control of the brutally hard stage nine with a savage solo attack on the first climb. Once free, he never let up and finished six minutes ahead of anyone else in L'Aquila.

Having wrought havoc on the race and deposed Giuseppe Olmo, taking from him the Maglia Rosa, he held on to the lead all the way to Milan, winning two more stages. It was an incredible success, but not one that Gino could savour. His brother Giulio died in a crash while racing in Tuscany just nine days later, an event that would have an ineradicable effect on Bartali, almost leading him to retire from racing and almost certainly intensifying his already staunch Catholic beliefs. After much soul-searching, he continued, a changed man but as powerful as ever. The Giro was his again in 1937, with four stages along the way, as well as a stage at the Tour de France, another Lombardia, his second national championship, and an array of other races. In 1938, he became Italy's second winner at the Tour de France.

So while the 1939 Giro della Toscana was the pair's first contest, the two riders at that point lived in very different worlds. It wouldn't be long, however, before Bartali would have to take notice of his young rival. Having impressed the management at Gino's Legnano team, Coppi was quickly signed up as a gregario, with the idea that he would make an able assistant to their Tuscan captain. Fausto, subordinate to no one, had other ideas.

A week after Germany began its invasion of France, the 28th Giro began in Milan. For obvious reasons, the peloton was almost exclusively Italian, with the winner of the last two editions, Bianchi's Giovanni Valetti, expected to be Bartali's main rival. But on just the second stage, Bartali came undone, crashing badly on the Passo della Scoffera after hitting a dog. Bullish as ever, he remounted and chased the peloton, but arrived in Genoa more than five minutes behind the winner, Pierino Favalli. Even injured, overturning such a lead wasn't beyond Bartali, who was, after all, a two-time Giro winner and the reigning Italian national champ. But there was another problem. His gregario, the young Coppi, had finished second, and was now on a par with Osvaldo Bailo and four other riders at the top of the GC. Over the following days, Bartali's injuries continued to trouble him and he couldn't keep pace with the leaders. Italy's most famous cyclist was out of the top 10, while his unknown 'helper' was in second, just a minute behind Favalli. Even as Favalli fell away and Enrico Mollo took control, Coppi remained in contention, looking like anything but someone else's assistant. Gianni Brera, one of the country's most formidable sports writers, would later say: 'Coppi was a cuckoo, born in the nest of a triumphant dove.'

Eberardo Pavesi, the Legnano boss, had a problem. It's the kind of predicament that every team manager has nightmares about: do you lose the race and keep faith with your star rider, or risk his wrath by backing someone else in the quest for the victory that your paymasters are screaming for? On stage 11, from Florence to Modena, Fausto made the decision for him. Getting from Tuscany to Emilia-Romagna required the race to traverse the Apennines, over the difficult climb to Abetone. The weather was horrific, and a cocktail of lightning storms, sleet and hail engulfed the peloton as it made its ascent. Coppi was part of a small breakaway that included Mollo and by the time they reached the Abetone climb, it was obvious. Pavesi hadn't found a gregario in Fausto, he'd found a champion. The young Piemontese was daunted neither by the occasion nor by the opposition: it was time to let him loose. The series of attacks that Coppi unleashed on his unsuspecting competitors that day have since become legendary, but at the time it was a revelation: this kid, unknown, as graceful as he was violent, leaving them all for dead to ride off alone and claim the Maglia Rosa. In the blink of an eye, the 20-year-old son of subsistence farmers became the darling of Italy.

Bartali battled on, patently unimpressed with his demotion,

but with an eye on the big mountains of the Dolomites and what he thought would be the inevitable collapse of his overly enthusiastic young companion. When that collapse came, however, Gino's reaction was unexpected, and the mark of a good man. After flatting early on stage 16, Bartali found young Coppi in crisis on the side of the road, suffering from stomach problems and having been dropped by his rivals. The Legnano captain coached him back to life, convinced him to remount and to respond to his inner doubts in the only way that he could, by salvaging his Giro. The pair flung themselves up the mountain in pursuit, railing against their great lost cause. Somehow, they erased most of the deficit, arriving in Pieve di Cadore three minutes behind the winner but only seconds behind Mollo. Gino's help kept Coppi in pink, and was one of several cordial moments that would make their rivalry all the more unique for its complexity.

The next day was another vital one in the creation of the Bartali-Coppi legend. The hardest of the race, it involved three of the Dolomites' most famed passes: the Falzarego, Pordoi and Sella. According to the most popular narrative, Pavesi went ahead of the peloton to a café at the top of Falzarego, where he told the barman to have two bottles of coffee ready for his two riders when they came over the pass. But how would the café owner know who to give it to? Simple, replied Pavesi. They'll be the first ones over, one will be wearing the Italian champion's Tricolore, and the other will be in the Maglia Rosa. The pair crested the mountain alone, never leaving one another's side. When one flatted, the other waited, and by the finish in Ortisei they had more than two minutes on Mollo. Bartali was rewarded with the win on the race's queen stage, and Coppi had built a commanding lead in the general classification that would see him safely to glory at Milan's Vigorelli velodrome four days later. What could so easily have been a nightmare for

Pavesi and Legnano had turned into a dream, albeit a brief one. The day after the Giro's finale, Mussolini marched his soldiers into France and Italy was plunged into war.

Coppi was conscripted for service before the 28th Giro had even begun, but his regiment gave him a deferment to allow him to compete, and upon his return to barracks, the magnanimity afforded to cycling's rising star endured. The regime in Italy was keen to keep up appearances at home and pushed for the continuation of sporting events right up until Mussolini's arrest, but holding a three-week stage race like the Giro, that covered thousands of kilometres and consumed huge fuel and food resources, was impossible. Smaller events carried on, and Coppi continued to race, beating Bartali to the 1941 Giro di Toscana and the 1942 national championships, before setting a new Hour Record of 45.798 kilometres on 7 November at Milan's Vigorelli, an event that the organisers timed to avoid the usual Allied bombing raids that had already damaged the velodrome. The day after, Allied troops began Operation Torch in Morocco and Algeria and at that point, Corporal Fausto Coppi of the 38th Infantry Regiment of the Ravenna Division received his orders. He was bound for the African front.

In Tuscany, meanwhile, Bartali stayed out of the war and, on the face of it, out of politics. He continued to train, spending long days in the saddle, criss-crossing Tuscany on its web of craggy, white gravel roads. Gino was probably the most famous man in Italy at that point, after Mussolini, and fame, coupled with his close connections to the Catholic Church, meant that few people were willing to risk the inevitable backlash that would come from harassing him. Little did they know that those ponderous rides had a purpose. Bartali had been approached by the Cardinal of Florence, Archbishop Elia Dalla Costa, who gave him a mission: to secretly smuggle documents in the seat-tube of his bicycle, destined for a network of partisans in Assisi who were using them to save the lives of Jewish families. By securing documents for a safe passage between the Repubblica Sociale Italiana, the puppet state run by the Nazis in the north of the country, and the Allied-controlled south, hundreds of people escaped to freedom. His involvement was to remain a secret for decades, even in his family, and it was only in his final years that Bartali eventually opened up about it. In 2013, 13 years after his death, the state of Israel declared him 'Righteous Among the Nations'.

Fausto spent most of his time in Africa as a British prisoner of war, followed by a stint as a driver working for the RAF in Naples. Upon his release, he found that his parents had invested his savings in war bonds while he was away, and so he returned to normal life a poor man. He initially returned to racing locally, competing in Campania and Lazio, before riding his bicycle back to Castellania on his own, through the wreckage of a country laid low by Allied bombing and a bitter civil war. To many, Coppi was post-war Italy in microcosm, an unwilling soldier, forced to fight someone else's war and now left alone to pick up the pieces. But he was also a superstar, the winner of the Giro d'Italia, robbed of some of his best years by the conflict. That dichotomy made him irresistible; he was at the same time both other-worldly and one of their own.

Thirteen months after the fall of the Reichstag in Germany and the execution of Mussolini on the banks of Lake Como, the Giro d'Italia returned and with it some semblance of normality. Or, as the Gazzetta colourfully put it: 'The people of Naples and Turin, of Lombardy and Lazio, of Veneto and Emilia, all Italians, many regions as part of a single civilisation and of a single heart, are all waiting for the Giro, the mirror in which they can recognise themselves again and smile.'

Unsurprisingly, organising a race amid the ruins of a world war was a logistical nightmare, but Armando Cougnet optimistically planned out 20 stages as best he could, and racing began on 15 June, a week after a national referendum had transformed Italy into a republic and sent the royal family packing. The country was still technically at war with the rest of Europe, so it was an all-Italian affair. But few cared about that: Bartali was there with Legnano and Pavesi, and Coppi came with his Bianchi team and a carte blanche to ride as he pleased. Both riders were in brilliant form, and their rivalry was already intense before the Giro got under way. Feigning illness at a race in Switzerland the month before, Gino had promised not to contest the sprint as long as Fausto didn't drop him before the finish. Then, in a very unchristian manner for such a pious man, he jumped Coppi and took the victory. The papers called that year's Corsa Rosa the *Giro della Rinascita*, the Giro of Rebirth, in celebration of Italy's new start. It could just as easily have been a reference to the renaissance of the battle between the nation's two greatest sportsmen.

Unexpectedly, for a race involving those two, the most romantic moment of that year's Giro involved neither. The plan for the 14th stage amounted to what was a ballsy, foolish move from Cougnet. Ignoring an official government statement – the fact that one was issued speaks volumes about the social and political importance of the race at the time – the route took the race from Rovigo to troublesome Trieste on the border with present-day Slovenia, which was, at the time, occupied by Yugoslavian troops. The city had once been an integral port for the Austro-Hungarian Empire, and cost the lives of hundreds of thousands of Italian soldiers in the First World War as they fought to reclaim it. Under Mussolini, its diverse demographic was rapidly and brutally Italianised, all foreign languages were banned, and citizens of Slavic origin were forced to change their names. So when Josip Tito's troops liberated it from Nazi control in 1945, they responded in kind. Thousands of Italian nationalists and anti-communists were imprisoned or murdered, while the western Allied troops stationed there looked on with trepidation. By 1946, it had become one of the emergent Cold War's most dangerous flash points.

Around 40 kilometres from the finish, the peloton was stopped with makeshift barricades and Slavic rebels throwing stones. There are several, no doubt embellished, versions of what happened next, but most agree that shots were fired and that Cougnet cancelled the stage. When news of the attack and the cancellation reached Trieste, however, riots erupted. And in the peloton, too, there was discontent, as several of the riders were from the area and felt very strongly about finishing in their home town as part of what they felt was their national race. Lead by Giordano Cottur, a Trieste native and one of the finest riders of the age, a debate began. After several hours of deliberation, it was decided that the stage would be annulled officially, but that anyone who wished to continue could do so, under armed guard. Seventeen bravely assented, and were duly loaded up into a US military transport vehicle and taken to the city limits to contest the final dramatic kilometres for the sake of honour (and the prize money, obviously). Cottur broke away immediately and rode into his home town a hero, with rapturous crowds overwhelming the small cadre of racers who had been courageous enough to come. Italy's biggest and best-loved celebration had come to Trieste, to its Italians, in spite of everything. Rarely has a sporting event made a bigger political, or poetic, statement. Writing in the *Gazzetta*, Bruno Roghi said: 'The gardens of Trieste have no more flowers. The bells of San Giusto cathedral no longer ring. The flags of the city no longer wave. The lips of Trieste have no more kisses. The flowers, the sounds, the waves, and the kisses have all been given to the Giro d'Italia.'

For our two protagonists, the race's key juncture came in

the Dolomites a couple of days later. Coppi, trailing in the GC after some initial difficulties but clearly getting better by the day, won the first big mountain stage, attacking on the Passo della Mauria. Bartali, however, had stayed with him and by finishing on the same time he moved into the Maglia Rosa, four minutes ahead of his gregario-turned-adversary. Coppi won again the next day, distancing the pack with a powerful ascent of the Falzarego, but it wasn't enough. Gino, thanks to the work of his teammates, was only a minute behind. Fausto ran out of spark by the final big climbing day to Trento, and couldn't make an attack stick. Thanks to his wins and the time bonuses they garnered, he was close, but not close enough. Bartali won his third Giro d'Italia by 47 seconds, having done enough in the mountains to limit his losses to the peerless Coppi. Two strokes of luck also helped. The first was when Cougnet decided against having a time trial – Coppi was by some margin the stronger against the clock. And the second was on stage five, when Coppi crashed and broke a rib. He still managed to win that's day's finish in Bologna, but for the ever-fragile Fausto, pain would catch up – throughout his career, it seemed sometimes the only thing that could catch him – as the race progressed.

Coppi would get his revenge the following spring, snatching the pink jersey from Bartali's back with a merciless attack on the Pordoi, but in order to narrate every battle between the two you'd need another book. And it would only be telling part of the story. Both lost time to the war, and there was an age gap, but statistically their encounters ended thus. In events they both started, Coppi won 69 to Bartali's 27. When neither won, the former finished ahead of the latter 171 times to 159. Coppi won five Giri, two Tours de France and two World Championships to Bartali's three Giri and two Tours. Bartali won seven of the races we now call monuments, though he never contested the northern classics like Paris–Roubaix, and Coppi won nine.

By the late 1940s, they'd become icons – in the true sense of the word – of Italian society and of the struggles with which it was grappling: morality and modernity, religion and social change, communism and the Christian centre. For the *Bartaliani* and *Coppiani*, they were more than bicycle racers. They were an integral part of their cultural identity.

Bartali symbolised continuity. His second Tour de France win, in 1948, came a decade after his first win, a record that still stands. It was also an achievement that some historians argue might have distracted sports-mad Italy just enough to avoid another civil war. He was the everyman; the very picture of small-town Italy, tough and reliable, and he was so popular among the faithful that his name was invoked by the Pope during sermons. Nicknames are a common thing in cycling, but rarely are they as laced with innuendo as the two monikers prescribed to Bartali. The common Italian suffix '-accio' is often used to imply that something is bad or has a wicked side, but also that someone is clever ... in a sly way. *Ginettaccio* summed up his character perfectly – the gruff, temperamental and demanding rider with a voice as gravelly as the dusty Tuscan back roads upon which he trained. Not a negative epithet in a country where street smarts and cunning are among the most prized of personality traits, but not exactly high praise either. And then there was his other side, Gino the Pious, which, depending on the speaker, could be taken as praise for his devotion to the church or a cheap dig at his religious zeal.

Though he came from poor, agrarian stock, Coppi exemplified the new, both the good and the bad of it. For one, he looked like a film star, enjoyed life's finer things, and was often pictured in one of the many glistening new cars that were rolling out of the factories in Turin. But like the country's economic recovery and many of the new moneyed classes, much of it was superficial. He never seemed totally at ease with himself in the same way that his rival did when he was pictured propped up in bed, smoking cigarettes, drinking wine and playing cards, looking more like a labourer than one of the world's great athletes. Like the future, Coppi was volatile and uncertain. Even at his most imperious, he was brittle. A spectacular success could be followed by agonising collapse. That was, for the most part, the arch of his career: a dizzying high giving way to a desolate descent.

Coppi was at the zenith of his powers in the late 1940s and early 1950s. His performance on stage 17 of the 1949 Giro d'Italia has become the stuff of legend, and was unlike anything that came before or since. Before the 254-kilometre stage from Cuneo to Pinerolo that took the peloton across into France and over a gruelling series of climbs – Maddalena, Vars, Izoard, Montgenèvre, and Sestriere – Fausto was trailing the Maglia Rosa Adolfo Leoni by 43 seconds. But the race's new director, Vincenzo Torriani, had planned the route with mayhem in mind, and that's exactly what he got.

The race left Cuneo in the cold and under driving rain, with the riders staring dead in the face of nine hours worth of hell. Coppi covered an early lone breakaway, before discarding the optimistic soloist before the top of the Maddalena. Bartali was forced to give chase, thinking that surely no one in their right mind would make their genuine play that early in the race's most challenging day. He must have thought his luck was in when he passed Coppi shortly after, dismounted on the side of the road while his mechanic saw to a problem with his chain, but that luck ran out not long after when Coppi caught and passed him. They had 190 kilometres to go. By Montgenèvre, Coppi's lead was more than six minutes on Bartali, the only rider who could even think of catching him. By Sestriere, he'd scratched out two more, and by the finish in Pinerolo, the gap was almost 12 minutes. The rest of the chasers arrived more than 19 minutes down. It was a massacre, and the Maglia was his; Gino was in second, but 23 minutes, a lifetime, behind him. As his friend Raphaël Géminiani used to say, you didn't need a stopwatch to time Coppi's lead in those days. The church bell tower would suffice.

A month later, with Bartali in support, Coppi would become the first rider ever to win a Giro-Tour double. He'd do it again in 1952, with a plethora of other titles in between. But the downward spiral had begun by then. During the 1951 Milano–Torino, Coppi's younger brother Serse crashed when his wheel caught a tram-track on the final straight of the race. He rode back to his hotel, but was rushed to hospital later that night, where he died in Fausto's arms of a brain haemorrhage. Serse had been a constant companion throughout his brother's life, his only real confidant, and it was something that Coppi never got over. Without his more exuberant brother to right him, he too often lost himself to self-doubt and his melancholic disposition.

There were marital problems too. Having married his wife Bruna in 1945 and fathered a daughter, Coppi scandalised Italy when he left his family for a married woman, Giulia Occhini, who was dubbed 'La Dama Bianca', the White Woman, by the press after being spotted with the Campionissimo wearing a white coat. Pitifully, Giulia's husband, a doctor by the name of Enrico Locatelli, was a huge Coppi fan and had introduced the pair in 1948. In a typically Italian paradox, adultery was both commonplace and frowned upon. It was also illegal, so when Locatelli refused to play the cuckold, the couple were arrested and Occhini was forced to live with family away from Fausto's reach. There was a show trial to appease the baying masses, now turned on their erstwhile idol, and the pair were given suspended sentences, with Coppi suffering the added indignity of having his passport confiscated and his entire deposition reported verbatim in the press. The couple were married in Mexico, unrecognised by the church, and had a child in Argentina, named Faustino, and everywhere they went, unscrupulous editors hounded them with no other end than the titillation of readers. The case exposed how out of touch Italy's legal and moral codes were with modern life and would eventually lead to change, but it was too little, too late, for Fausto and Giulia.

Coppi's last day in the Maglia Rosa came in 1954, after the opening stage's team time trial. It was the same year that Bartali retired. Coppi's career declined gracefully, occasionally showing flashes of the champion he had been, and over time most people forgave his private failings. As they aged, the two rivals, never enemies, seemed to become friends. There was a Team Coppi vs. Team Bartali football match in Milan played out in front of thousands, with Giuseppe Meazza, the most famous footballer in Italy before the war, as referee. And in the late 1950s, the pair would occasionally appear on Italian television, like a bizarre comedy double act. On a famous programme of the time, Il Musichiere, the two even sang together, with Coppi poking fun at Bartali for losing and Bartali joking about how many drugs Coppi took. How times have changed.

All of Coppi's life had been like something out of Hollywood or, more fittingly, Cinecittà, the celebrated heart of Italian cinema situated on the outskirts of Rome. Sadly, it was not destined for a happy ending. At the end of 1959, Coppi joined Raphaël Géminiani and several other riders for a cycling and hunting trip to Burkina Faso at the invitation of the country's president. He shared a room with his friend, and both caught malaria. Géminiani was quickly diagnosed upon his return to France, and made a full recovery. Coppi's doctor insisted it was the flu, and through his neglect condemned the champion of champions to an early grave. More than 50,000 were in attendance at his funeral, swarming around the hearse as it made its final ascent to Castellania. Italy was in mourning for one of its truly universal heroes. He had been, in the end, something for everyone. A rags-to-riches fairy tale. A scandal. An imperfect man and impeccable champion. He was, as Gianni Mura, one of Italy's best known and most talented sports writers, put it, 'The perfect myth'.

7

MAGNI: IL TERZO UOMO

Three is a number synonymous with Fiorenzo Magni. He won three Giri d'Italia, three editions of the Ronde van Vlaanderen, three Italian National Championships, three Giri del Piemonte and triumphed three times at the prestigious, but now sadly defunct, Trofeo Baracchi, a two-man time trial beloved by Jacques Anquetil, Eddy Merckx, Francesco Moser, and Laurent Fignon. To do all of that in a career filled with a profusion of other victories would be a feat in itself, but to do it during his particular era was nothing short of extraordinary. That's because, for all the happy trinities in Magni's life, his career was defined by a different kind of triplicity. He had the unfortunate task of carving out a career for himself in a triumvirate with Gino Bartali and Fausto Coppi. In the era of cycling's greatest duality, he was Il Terzo Uomo, the Third Man.

Magni was born on 20 December 1920, to Giuseppe and Giulia in the small Tuscan town of Vaiano, in the hills north of Florence. It was not an easy childhood. Aged just four, he almost lost a leg to amputation after being incorrectly diagnosed by his local doctor and was only spared that tragic maiming by a last-minute operation in the Tuscan capital. His father, a carter who transported goods for local farms and businesses and who introduced him to cycling, died in an accident when Fiorenzo was just 17, leaving his son to take over the humble family business and support his mother and sister, Fiorenza.

He managed to still find time for the bike, and began racing as a teenager, but had barely begun to make a name for himself locally when war broke out across Europe. Like so many cyclists before him, Magni applied to join the Bersaglieri. In a blessed twist of fate for the future champion, he was allowed leave to compete in a race while his unit left without him for the recently conquered Albania. Their ship was sunk on the way, leaving no survivors. After that, he served in Rome and then in Tuscany, before moving his family north to Monza, not far from Milan, in 1944. That period in Tuscany has long been the subject of intense debate, because in common with much of what happened in wartime Italy, Magni's politics and his actions in uniform are still far from clear. In July 1943, with Allied troops rapidly pressing north through the country after the invasion of Sicily, the Fascist Grand Council voted to remove Mussolini from office before having him arrested. By September, an armistice with the British and Americans had been signed, but when Il Duce was sprung from prison by German special forces in a raid code-named 'Operation Eiche', the Repubblica Sociale Italiana was set up as a puppet regime in Nazi-occupied northern Italy. Magni, who would always maintain that he had little choice in the matter if he didn't want to risk the firing squad, remained a part of the National Republican Guard, Mussolini's new gendarmerie, and in January 1944 would find himself at the centre of the action as the first shots were fired between partisans and Fascists in Italy's nascent civil war. The Battle of Valibona began when fascist troops discovered and surrounded a small group of resistance fighters led by Lanciotto Ballerini, a prominent figure in the guerrilla movement. After several hours of fighting, a number of the rebels, Ballerini included, lay dead while more were taken off to prison and tortured. Magni's part in all of this is unclear.

Some historians claim documentary proof that the cyclist was an eager supporter of the Fascists, and that he even went so far as to work with notorious gangs who conspired with Nazi troops to capture and terrorise Jewish families and enemies of the regime. More recently, however, evidence has emerged, in the form of official documents, showing that Magni, far from being a fascist colluder, worked with the partisans throughout his time in uniform, risking his own safety to distribute documents and anti-fascist literature to liberation forces. Whatever the truth of the matter, with the fall of fascism and the end of the war, young Magni was again on the move, fearing the popular backlash against anyone thought to have served the regime too willingly. He hopped around the south of the peninsula before eventually facing trial for his part in the massacre at Valibona, as tensions in the war-torn country mounted between those eager to get to the truth, and those simply desperate for vengeance. Bartali was called to the court to give evidence, but didn't show. However, another important name in Italian cycling, Alfredo Martini, who would later serve as the national team manager for almost 20 years during the Azzurri's most dominant period, testified in Magni's favour.

Martini, a proud communist all his life, must have known something about the putative fascist who would later become his teammate and friend. Speaking in old age of their relationship, Magni would say: 'Men are more than their ideas.' The prosecutor had called for a 30-year sentence for those involved, but Magni, according to testimonies, had played no role, and was eventually acquitted of any wrongdoing in 1947, in part thanks to the Togliatti Amnesty, the post-war government's attempt at nationwide reconciliation. Later that year, he married Liliana Calò, a woman who played an integral role in his life both private and professional, and with whom he would spend the rest of his days. He was just about to turn 27, and for the first time in his life, could finally concentrate on racing.

The Italian cycling federation had rescinded his licence in 1946 due to the claims of fascist collusion – one wonders how much anyone in the upper offices of that organisation had done against Mussolini's regime – but now that he was free, Magni signed for the Wilier Triestina team alongside the aforementioned Martini and Trieste's hero, Giordano Cottur, and began competing in earnest in 1947. He had raced during the war, winning his first Giro del Piemonte in 1942 and making the top 10 twice at Milano–Sanremo, but the 30th edition of the Giro was his first. He finished a credible ninth, but almost 35 minutes behind the winner, Coppi. There was plenty of room for improvement, and he proved it 12 months later. The 1948 Giro was 4,164 kilometres of pure drama, and Magni was at the heart of it.

Both Bartali and Coppi had come with plenty of firepower, in the Legnano and Bianchi teams respectively, but the pair inexplicably let Magni's Wilier Triestina teammate Cottur get away on the very first stage, gifting him the pink jersey and a lead in the general classification of more than nine minutes. Both the Uomo di Ferro and L'Airone – Coppi was often likened to a heron by journalists because of his long limbs, beak-like nose, and the way in which he sometimes seemed to take flight – were in fine form, Coppi having won Milano–Sanremo by more than five minutes that spring, and the pair must have thought it would end up a duel between them once the race reached the high mountains in its final week, but even so, allowing a team as talented as Wilier Triestina such a lead early on was a serious, and uncharacteristic, blunder.

Over the next few stages, they closed the gap, but after eight stages, the only man less than five minutes behind Cottur was Martini. Stage nine's mountainous, coast-to-coast trek across the Apennines from Bari to Naples changed all that, but not in favour of Coppi or Bartali. An early breakaway escaped, and no one paid it any heed. Over the course of the day's 306 kilometres, the main contenders were happy to mark one another closely, and almost nine hours after leaving the Adriatic coast, they arrived on the Tyrrhenian Sea together. The problem was that they did so 13 minutes after the stage winner, Nedo Logli. Vito Ortelli, who had been in the break too, took over the GC lead, and a minute and 33 seconds behind him was Magni. With one fearless, enervating move, he had put himself in contention. It was the kind of move that would come to distinguish his career.

An untimely mechanical cost Ortelli dearly on stage 14, when he lost sight of Magni's group on the way to Udine. The 27-year-old Tuscan now lead the race by just under a minute from the unheralded Ezio Cecchi – the first of the big names, Cottur, was more than three minutes behind – but with difficult days in the mountains to come, that margin was anything but secure. In fact, the very next day he lost three minutes to Ortelli, Coppi, Bartali and a small group of other riders on the Sappada climb in Veneto and found himself out of the Maglia Rosa just as quickly as he'd claimed it. The following day, Coppi decided that it was time for a masterclass, and on the short, 90-kilometre stage to Cortina d'Ampezzo, he managed to put three minutes and 32 seconds into Bartali and the chasing pack. It moved him into the top 10, and with a gruelling 160-kilometre day to Trento to follow the next morning, a route that included the Falzarego and Pordoi passes, the Campionissimo was now back in contention. Stage 17, another lesson. Coppi beat Ortelli, Cottur and Magni by two and a half minutes and finished more than seven minutes ahead of his great rival Bartali, who had a nightmare of a day with two flats during the crucial climbs. The Bianchi captain was now in third overall, but Magni was back in pink, albeit contentiously.

Magni was never a bad climber, but he was never first class, either. When he won, he did it thanks to his unpredictable opportunism, his skill in adverse conditions, the aggressive vigour that he injected into every solo attack, and his peerless descending ability. And, every so often, his willingness to push the boundaries. Most of the time, the boundaries in question were those of human endurance, but in this case it was the rules of the game that he wished to test. Wilier, it transpired, had transported their own fans deep into the mountains, leaving them perfectly positioned to push the team's riders on key sections of the most difficult climbs. In the days of unpaved climbs, limited gearing and burdensome bicycles, getting a helping hand from a biased fan was commonplace, but the scale of Wilier's swindle shocked everyone.

Coppi was apoplectic. He'd seen his lead on the Pordoi demolished by blatant cheating and demanded that the organisers throw Magni out of the race, or at least penalise him heavily. Armando Cougnet and his assistant, the young Vincenzo Torriani, were not so troubled by the unedifying display. Greedy for a spectacular end to the race that would sell more papers, they opted for a more placatory approach and docked him two minutes. Conveniently enough, that left Magni in the lead by the tantalising margin of 11 seconds over Cecchi, with two stages left to play. Disgusted, Bianchi retired from the race in protest. Negotiations went on through the night at the team's hotel, but Coppi was adamant and could not be reconciled. When the press and the fans noticed that the country's most famous sportsman was no longer present the next morning, there was bedlam. Bartali would go on to win one of the greatest Tours of all time that summer, including six stages, but he was off the pace at the Giro and with Coppi gone, there was no one to stop Fiorenzo taking the glory, such as it was. He maintained his lead on Cecchi – still the smallest in Giro history – and rolled across the line at Milan's Vigorelli velodrome two days later to a cacophony of boos and hisses. La Stampa called it a 'Miserable End', while the journalist Giuseppe Ambrosini, who would later become the director of the Gazzetta dello Sport, reported the abuse that the winner had received, including banners on the roadside that read 'Long live Coppi, champion of cycling – Down with Magni, champion of pushing.' Some reporters, openly hostile to the Tuscan because of his connection to Valibona, dismissed his victory entirely, while the violent heckling in the velodrome was said to have reduced Magni to tears, tainting the race and exposing just how caustic Italian society could be. Ambrosini eloquently opined that it was a 'melancholic epilogue to a flawed Giro'.

The following spring, Magni set off with just one gregario for the Ronde van Vlaanderen. It was his second visit to Belgium, having crashed out the year before, but learning from race reports and from his own experience, he made sure that his bike was specially prepared for the cobbles with padding in the bar-tape, thicker and heavier tubulars and wooden-rimmed wheels, which he thought more flexible and trustworthy on the setts. Beating 17 other riders in a massive sprint to become only the second foreigner to triumph in Flanders, after Switzerland's Heiri Suter who won in 1923, Magni became an instant hero. The prolific novelist and sports reporter Emilio De Martino romanticised the victory, describing how Magni rode 'alone against 200 others, alone against the terrible cobbles, the wind, the doubters, alone against the wickedness of man'. Illness kept him from the Giro, which was won that year by Coppi, but he was fit in time for the Tour and he lined up as part of the Campionissimo's contingent. In 1950, Fiorenzo cemented his legend in northern Europe – they still call him the Lion of Flanders – by winning his second Ronde and coming third at Paris–Roubaix. At the Giro, he managed a typically impulsive solo win on stage 16 to Campobasso, leaving everyone in his dust, but by his standards it was a quiet race. He found his form at the Tour, only to be robbed of a chance to win in France when Bartali demanded that the Italian team retire in protest after they'd been attacked by feral fans in the mountains. Every time he went to France, Fiorenzo would wear the Maillot Jaune, but never did he have a better opportunity to take it home. The history of cycling is full of riders whining over what might have been, but Magni never complained about that July, saying time and again that he believed in Bartali and that in life, some things were more important than trophies.

Magni was a rider full of fireworks and, at his best, his attacks were akin to theatre. On 1 April 1951, he attacked the Ronde peloton with 75 kilometres still to go, but it was a serious manoeuvre. He won by five and a half minutes, along the way collecting around 30,000 francs in bonus prizes – in those days, enough to buy a large house. Always shrewd with money, that same year he opened up a motorcycle dealership that was later expanded to include cars. Those business interests didn't get in the way of his racing, however, and he also won Milano–Torino, the Giro del Lazio and the Giro di Romagna before lining up for the Ganna team at the 34th Giro d'Italia against Coppi, who was still not quite recovered after breaking his collarbone in March, and Bartali, who was just shy of his 37th birthday, walking with a limp and starting to show signs of rust. The Lion of Flanders was about to unexpectedly find himself pitched against a Belgian hero.

Rik van Steenbergen was a force of nature in the northern classics and one-day races. He was world champion three times, and won twice at Paris–Roubaix, the Ronde, and La Flèche Wallonne. And he wasn't just about the quality races, either. In a career spanning almost two decades, he was infamously more interested in the lucrative appearance fees promised by smaller races and track events, and though accounts differ wildly, reasonable estimates total his wins at more than 1,000. Lamentably, he would lose his fortune to gambling and poor life choices in a long and unhappy retirement, but in 1950 he was at the height of his powers, and so he came to Italy to prove that he could do it in stage races too.

Following the tale of what happened at this Giro requires some concentration. Van Steenbergen duly took the first stage to Turin, as Bartali crashed badly, losing a quarter of an hour and all hope of winning the GC. Magni overturned his lead the following day, putting almost two minutes into the Belgian in a race over the mountains to the Ligurian coast. Three days later, he lost the lead again when a surprising breakaway laid waste to the main group and put the Swiss rider Fritz Schaer in the lead, with Van Steenbergen just over a minute behind. Stage six's monstrous 83-kilometre time trial around Perugia, not a part of Italy known for being flat, gave Coppi the chance to show that, even when not fully fit, he was still a force to be reckoned with. The Piemontese was more than a minute quicker than France's great hope, Louison Bobet, and more than two ahead of Magni, who he joined level in third place in the general classification.

The following stage to Rome saw another impressive breakaway, but this time all of the main contenders, except for poor Schaer, made it across the line at the same time, putting Van Steenbergen back in pink – for 24 hours. In a race that was full of champions and lacking in anyone who could put one over on his rivals, the Belgian capitulated on stage eight to Naples, falling to fifth in the overall rankings and somehow

1. This 'Viva Coppi' pennant is from 1954, when the Campionissimo was the reigning world champion and had already won the Tour de France twice and the Giro five times.

2. From the beginning, the Giro was hugely popular with the Italian public. Here, enormous crowds gather in Florence's Parco delle Cascine to welcome the first edition of the race in 1909.

3. '3,000 kilometres – 25,000 lire in prizes.'
The front page of the Gazzetta dello Sport on
24 August 1908 announces the inaugural Giro d'Italia,
promising improbable distances and a fortune for the
winner.

4. Armando Cougnet, the first Patron of the Giro, was
only 18 years old when he joined the editorial staff of
the Gazzetta in 1898.

5. A stonemason by trade, Luigi Ganna shot to national fame when he won the maiden Giro d'Italia in 1909, seen here with Carlo Galetti to his left. Known as 'the Squirrel of the Canals', Galetti would win the Giro in 1910, 1911 and as part of the Atala team in 1912.

6. Alfredo Binda, one of the most dominant riders in cycling history, pictured with Emilio Colombo, the editor of the Gazzetta dello Sport. The pair had a difficult relationship, as Binda's superiority often lead to boring races – and more importantly, poor newspaper sales.

7. Luigi Ganna, Eberardo Pavesi, Giovanni Micheletto, Carlo Galetti and Natale Bosco pictured during the 1912 Giro.

8. The Bersaglieri are a high-mobility unit in the Italian armed forces, famous for the long black plumage that decorates their hats, and for their distinctive, rapid marching style. At the turn of the century it was common for these soldiers to go to battle with a bicycle, and in 1912 they even entered an offical Italian Army team into the Giro.

9. Costante Girardengo went from working in a factory in Genoa to becoming one of the first truly rich professional athletes. It was said that in the 1920s, to most Italians he was more recognisable than the country's fascist leader, Benito Mussolini.

10. On top of being the world's best cyclist, Alfredo Binda was an accomplished trumpeter and on at least one occasion he entertained fans after winning a race by borrowing an instrument and treating the finish-line crowd to an impromptu concert.

11. Giovanni Brunero was the first rider to win the Giro three times, in 1921, 1922 and 1926. He died a young man, aged 39, after being ill for the final few years of his life.

12. Alfredo Binda was by some margin the more successful, but the tifosi preferred Learco Guerra, the man they called 'The Human Locomotive,' because he was the only rider capable of competing with the Campionissimo.

13. Alfonsina Strada competed in the 1924 edition of the race, making her the only woman to ever ride the Giro. She was so popular that along the route she stopped to sign autographs and hand out photographs of herself.

14. Ottavio Bottecchia survived poverty, World War I and malaria before becoming the first Italian to win the Tour de France. When his bloodied corpse was found by the roadside in 1934, it was rumoured to be the work of fascist thugs.

allowing Magni to turn a deficit of one minute 47 seconds into a two-minute lead. Fiorenzo's tenacity kept him in the jersey for a few more days, but the better climbers had their way with him on stage 12, an uphill time trial to San Marino. Giancarlo Astrua, a capable but unspectacular rider from north of Turin, won the day and took the GC lead by 18 seconds. By the following evening, Van Steenbergen was back, organising an attack on the way to Bologna that gave the win to Luciano Maggini, who had been a teammate of Fiorenzo's at Wilier back in 1948. The Belgian now had a four-minute lead on Astrua and more on Magni.

It was, without question, a commanding lead, but Van Steenbergen was not made for the mountains and that's exactly where they were headed next. On the first day in the Dolomites, from Trieste to Cortina d'Ampezzo, he surprised everyone. Coppi and Bobet fought for the win, but both were well off the GC pace. Magni followed them across the line half a minute later, with Bartali a minute behind him, but the big shock came when the tall, muscular classics specialist from Flanders rolled in not far behind. He may have lost time but he earned the respect of everyone who'd assumed he was incapable of climbing. Van Steenbergen was still in pink, but Magni was only 90 seconds behind him, and there were still two more alpine days to go. Stage 18 was truncated by snow, cutting out three serious ascents and in theory playing into the hands of the leader. Had the stage not been shortened, Coppi might have turned the whole race on its head, because he looked like a man reborn. Without a serious gradient upon which to turn the screw, however, he couldn't shake the best climbers or build a big enough gap in front of Van Steenbergen and Magni. On the day's final descent, Magni played his hand. Truly brilliant descenders are a rare strain, but when it came to going downhill, the Lion of Flanders was a thoroughbred. Van Steenbergen tried to hold his wheel as Magni took incredible risks, but eventually trepidation set in and all was lost. In those moments, on the knife edge between control and catastrophe, racers need guts and preternatural bike-handling abilities. Fiorenzo had both in spades. He caught Coppi before the finish in Bolzano, lost the sprint, but gained the lead. Van Steenbergen's nerves cost him more than three minutes. Koblet, ever popular, ever charming, pleased the Swiss crowds the following day with a solo win as the race crossed the northern border, but it was the Italian fans who had the most to be happy about, as Magni finished in Milan that Sunday with a lead of one minute and 46 seconds over his foreign rival. This time, they greeted his victory with cheers.

Magni turned 31 at the end of that year, but raced with the hunger of a much younger rider and the wins kept coming. In the early 1950s, he was prolific the length and breadth of Italy, beating Coppi and the declining Bartali on numerous occasions, and recording victories at important events like the Giro di Romagna, the Giro del Veneto, the Giro della Toscana and the Giro del Piemonte, one of his personal favourites. He also dominated the once-prestigious Roma–Napoli–Roma stage race, winning several stages and consecutive GC titles in 1952 and 1953. A third Giro, however, eluded him. Coppi was peerless in the 35th and 36th editions, and Carlo Clerici won a lifeless race in 1954 while the rest of the peloton protested over their conditions and payment.

Against that background of rider unrest, the most remarkable achievement of Magni that year happened off the bike, and would turn out to have a much greater impact on the sport as a whole than any grand tour victory ever could. Post-war Italy was a country in the middle of upheaval, and not just politically. It had gone from being the continent's richest country during the Middle Ages to being one of its poorest, and it was by far the weakest member of the European Coal and Steel Community, the precursor to the European Union, when it was formed in 1952. As the US flooded Europe with billions of dollars in financial aid through the Marshall Plan, however, the economy was revitalised and modernised within a few short years, seeing annual growth of around 6 per cent for two decades. What had been a nation of anachronistic farming, crippling poverty and limited education – the average Italian adult had less than four years of schooling in 1950 – quickly became one of the leading lights in western Europe's economic renaissance, during a period that Italian historians call Il miracolo economico, the Economic Miracle.

In a 1963 speech, the American president John F. Kennedy called Italy's recovery 'one of the most remarkable phenomena in the post-war period', remarking also that its transformation from devastated backwater to industrial powerhouse was 'unmatched in the western world'. Rapid industrialisation and urbanisation saw it transformed into a consumerist economy, and by the 1960s, Italian companies were market leaders. Fiat was Europe's biggest car manufacturer, fashion had come to the fore, and with the help of a burgeoning golden age in Italian cinema, the Bel Paese became a global symbol of modernity and style. The nation's disparate regions became easily accessible for the first time, too, thanks to ambitious infrastructure spending and projects like the Autostrada del Sole, that was completed in just eight years despite involving more than 750 kilometres of road between Milan and Naples, 38 tunnels, 115 bridges and, bizarrely, five churches.

For the average man in the street, this was a good thing, but for professional bike riders it posed a serious problem. Until the early 1950s, the sport had been funded by bicycle manufacturers, desperately trying to sell their wares. But with the continent's rapid modernisation, the bike was no longer the proletarian transportation of choice, and cheap offerings from the likes of Fiat, Vespa and Lambretta offered even the lower classes a faster, sexier way of getting from A to B. Bike sales went through the floor, with some estimates showing a drop of more than 60 per cent by the end of the decade. The blow to the big bike companies wasn't quite fatal, but they were going to have to be a lot more careful with the purse strings from that point on and could no longer afford to fund cycling teams – especially not when the likes of Coppi and Magni could command huge salaries and bonuses.

Pino Ganna, son of Luigi, the Giro's first winner, was in charge of his father's company by this stage and, by extension, the team that it sponsored. But by the end of 1953, Ganna was feeling the financial pressure and so decided against renewing contracts with Magni and his gregari for the following season. For a rider like the Lion of Flanders, this wasn't necessarily a problem because several other teams would have been happy to take him. What caused him to lose some sleep was the thought that his teammates might lose their jobs, not to mention that he'd have very little bargaining power with which to negotiate his own deal. Thinking creatively, Fiorenzo contacted a cosmetics company, Nivea, and proposed that they sponsor the team along with Fuchs, a bicycle manufacturer. They were delighted to be the first with a foot in the door and quickly coughed up around 20 million lire for the honour. Initially, the move was met with resistance from the wider cycling world, but when Adriano Rodoni, the president of the Italian cycling federation, Vincenzo Torriani, the new director of the Giro, and even Coppi took Magni's side, the matter was settled and professional sport never looked back.

In May of 1954, the grizzled, balding 33-year-old Magni lined up at the start of the 38th Giro in a distinctive royal blue jersey advertising women's facial cream. After the protests of the year before, Torriani had taken the riders' concerns on board and had cut the overall distance from an insane 4,337 kilometres – the longest Giro of all time – to a more manageable 3,873. Clerici, now a naturalised Swiss citizen, was back with his friend Hugo Koblet, and there was notable muscle from France too, with the likes of Raphaël Géminiani and Jean Dotto, the first Frenchman to win the Vuelta a España. Belgium's Rik Van Looy was also in attendance making his grand tour debut, but he hadn't yet developed into the powerful stage hunter who would twice be world champion and become the first to win all of cycling's five Monuments. Fiorenzo and Coppi, now a duo since Bartali's retirement, were the favourites. Fausto was in terminal decline, but he arrived to the race in good shape and no one was willing to discount the most successful rider of all time.

Magni took control early on, but it was Gastone Nencini, an eccentric young pro from Tuscany riding his second Giro, who surprised everyone by giving as good as he got to the Italian old guard and the likes of Clerici and Géminiani. After a win on stage nine to Rome, he was in fifth, but just 18 seconds behind the Maglia Rosa and clearly riding into form. Fiorenzo lost a minute and a half the following day in a difficult circuit race around the Castelli Romani, the hilltop towns just south of the Italian capital, giving the GC lead to the workmanlike Bruno Monti, with Géminiani and Nencini breathing down his neck. A day later, Monti lost eight minutes on the way to Naples and the Frenchman was in control, two seconds ahead of Nencini. Magni was left adrift, two and a half minutes behind. Not much changed as the race wound its way back north towards the Dolomites, and considering his age and his lacklustre climbing skills, things weren't looking great for the Lion of Flanders. By stage 18, Nencini was in pink and, as a capable climber and a fearless descender, thoroughly looking forward to the mountains.

Then, two things happened to seal the boisterous young rider's fate. First, he offended Coppi by marking him the whole way up the Passo Rolle climb before jumping him just before the summit to claim the mountain bonus. An impetuous move that lacked class in the eyes of the Campionissimo, this wasn't the done thing for the Maglia Rosa, especially not against a rider of Coppi's stature. And second, Fiorenzo Magni came up with a plan.

A large part of his brilliance had always come from his unwillingness to accept defeat, and it wasn't for nothing that he was often referred to as a *Toscanaccio*, a tough old Tuscan bastard. Stage 20 of the 1955 Giro was a perfect expression of that spirit. Knowing the area well, he picked the most battered stretch of road he could think of and earmarked it for an attack. Then, he got his mechanic to set up his bike for a northern classic like Flanders or Roubaix, before calling on Alfredo Martini and the rest of his team to inform them that, on his honour, the Giro was his, so they'd better rest up, because the next day was going to be hell. After that, it was time to make some deals. Koblet was nowhere near the rider he had been, but he couldn't be overlooked either, so he was promised the final stage win in Milan, as long as he sat up and soft pedalled when he saw Magni spring his attack. After that, it was simply a matter of appealing to Coppi's wounded pride. In return for his services, he was assured of the stage victory, and a chance to teach the young interloper a valuable lesson.

The Giro's penultimate stage started badly for the foredoomed Nencini. That crash was the least of his worries. As the road deteriorated, his team was strung out by fatigue and by punctures until the man in pink was left alone. Seeing his prey friendless and exposed, Magni burst to the front, fuelled by raging determination, and Coppi followed. Everyone else just let them go. Before long the peloton was out of sight and Nencini was out of luck, faced with 170 kilometres of solo racing against two of the sport's most gifted and most ruthless competitors. Radios across the country buzzed with the news. Magni and Coppi, the tough and the talented, were at it again. They'd ambushed the Giro with a brilliant, ruthless display of cunning and heart. People flooded out of their homes onto the roadside to see their stars, fading but not yet extinguished, cast their long shadows over everyone else one last time. Coppi would never win another stage of the Giro, but for one more day at least, he was a champion. Magni took the Maglia Rosa, 13 seconds ahead of his old foe in second, with a tearful Nencini four minutes behind. And the next day, Koblet was rewarded at the Vigorelli. Fiorenzo had kept his word to everyone, especially himself. At 34 years, 6 months and 29 days, he remains the race's oldest ever winner.

Magni was never as popular as Coppi or Bartali. His personality was too abrasive, his style too rough, his past too divisive. The blemish of his fascist youth followed him into old age, and when the regional government used his image to promote the Giro in 2009, protest among locals forced a change. During his career, some hostile journalists described him as a despot with his teammates – as if Coppi or Bartali was any better – and others accused him of using his gregari to pull him like sleigh-dogs in the opening kilometres of every race. Two of his Giri were won by the slimmest of margins, using tactics that weren't to everyone's taste. He wasn't as handsome as Fausto, didn't dress as well or play to the crowds, and he started to go bald in his twenties. He lacked the old-fashioned stature and strong morals of Gino. But he had his own gruff charm, and over the years, opinions softened. His was an inspirational tale for anyone up against impossible odds. And who doesn't like a story like that? One of the most often cited events of his colourful career came towards the end of it, in the 1956 Giro. Having broken his collarbone on stage 12 to Livorno, the doctors advised him to retire from the race. They wanted him in a cast, but he wanted to race. Bandaged, he continued, only to lose almost all the strength in his left arm – meaning he couldn't pull the bars while he climbed. The solution? His mechanic, Faliero Masi, tied a piece of inner tube around the handlebars so that he could pull with his teeth. The day after that, another crash broke his humerus and he passed out from the pain. Waking up in an ambulance, he flew into a fit and demanded to be let out so that he could continue. That left four more days of suffering, including two brutal mountain stages. He finished second on the Stelvio. And on stage 19, as most of the peloton froze or quit or both, he pressed on, incredulous at the fact that the Maglia Rosa had abandoned. Some 43 riders survived and made it to the final finish two days later in Milan, but only one of them with a pair of broken bones: Magni was second, three minutes behind Charly Gaul.

It was impossible not to admire that spirit, and, as time passed and the protagonists of that era along with it, Italy's cycling fans began to cherish Magni as a precious link to that special generation. He was a regular fixture at his car dealership until his death, lively into his nineties and happy to welcome anyone who cared to talk about the good old days.

In typical fashion, his death came as unexpectedly and as suddenly as his attacks once had, six decades prior. Magni died of an aneurism on 19 October 2012, after being taken to hospital the night before. His funeral was held in the Duomo of Monza, where he'd married Liliana 65 years earlier. And it was packed to the rafters with the great and the good. His old friend Alfredo Martini gave a touching eulogy to a man he said was universally loved: 'A great light has been extinguished,' mourned the 91-year-old elder statesman of Italian cycling from the pulpit, 'but we do not go on in the dark. His examples of honesty, intelligence, and steadfastness remain with us to light the way.' And with the Tricolore jersey draped over his coffin, the basilica was rightly filled with applause rather than sobs. He had passed away just short of his 92nd birthday, 12 years after Bartali and a lifetime after Coppi. Third again, but this time a willing runner-up.

PASSO DELLO STELVIO, TRENTINO-ALTO ADIGE

With two stages left of the 1953 Giro d'Italia, the race for the Maglia Rosa was over. Even Fausto Coppi thought so. Switzerland's Hugo Koblet, the Giro champion three years previously and one of the few men who could hold a candle to the Campionissimo, had been in pink since the eighth stage and looked unbeatable. Coppi's Bianchi team had thrown all they had at him, but Koblet still led by a couple of minutes.

But even as Coppi resigned himself to second, those closest to him weren't ready to give up. According to this tale's most popular telling, his loyal gregario, Ettore Milano, took it upon himself to do some detective work. As Koblet signed autographs and posed for pictures, Milano asked if he might have one taken with the champion for himself, asking him to remove his sunglasses under the pretext that he'd be more recognisable in the photograph. The Swiss amiably obliged, and unwittingly reignited Coppi's challenge, because underneath the dark shades lurked darker eyes. He hadn't slept. He was vulnerable. The 36th edition of the Giro was not as lost as it had seemed. Milano wasted no time in delivering the fruits of his espionage back to his captain.

Enter the Stelvio. Stage 20 from Bolzano in Alto Adige to Bormio in Lombardy was short for those days – a mere 125 kilometres – but its brevity was fooling no one. The route involved a new climb, more than 24 kilometres long, with 1,808 metres of altitude gain. A great unknown, but potentially the perfect grandstand for Italy's grandest talent.

The Bianchi team started to turn the screw early, like picadors wearing down a bull for the expectant matador. In the foothills and the lower slopes around Trafoi, Coppi's lieutenants tore away at the race leader's resolve until eventually, struggling with the Stelvio, his incessant rivals, and perhaps the weight of expectation, Koblet cracked. Wavering in a bend, he lost a bike length. Then two. Coppi took flight, some 11 kilometres from the top, wringing everything he could out of his body and his bike, churning a 46 x 23 gear and grinding his opponent into pieces. After a hair-raising descent into Bormio, during which he crashed, the Italian won the stage by almost three and a half minutes, enough to finish the following afternoon's final ride to Milan with an 89-second lead over the Swiss to take Giro number five – a victory that his countrymen would call 'Coppi's fifth symphony'.

Witnesses on the mountain that day, observing the stricken, desolate Koblet being escorted up the final kilometres by two police motorcycles, likened it to a funeral procession. Even the victor would later say that the effort had almost killed him. In its debut appearance, the Stelvio had left an indelible mark on the race and on the race's most iconic champion. And as a mark of respect to that transcendent performance, to this day we still refer to the Giro's highest point as the 'Cima Coppi' – the Coppi Peak.

Built in just five years and opened in 1825, the Passo dello Stelvio is perhaps the closest a road engineer will ever come to genuinely artistic expression. Carlo Donegani, a native of

Brescia, was employed by the Austrian crown to connect its newly acquired province of Lombardy to the rest of the Habsburg Empire. The Italian's solution was a 49-kilometre tour de force connecting the Valtellina valley with the Val Venosta.

From its more recognisable, picturesque side, the SS38 climbs from Ponte di Stelvio at an average gradient of around 7.5 per cent, maxing out at just over 9 per cent, two thirds of the way up. Donegani used 48 tight hairpins to conquer the mountain's eastern face, in a feat of genius that somehow manages to combine the potential of human ingenuity with the raw power of nature, and in doing so, elevate and honour them both.

The Bormio side is not to be scoffed at either, with gradients above 12 per cent in places along the 21.9-kilometre escalation that gains 1,560 metres in total. The Giro has tackled this face on several occasions, but it is more famous and feared as a descent, not least because of its five tunnels. That dive into total darkness is a real test of nerve at speed – especially for those frozen, esurient riders ravaged by the climb and desperate for the deliverance from misery that only the finish line below can offer.

Usurped as Europe's highest mountain pass by the Col d'Iseran in 1937, Donegani's serpentine masterpiece remains cycling's most iconic climb and though the aforementioned French road might be 12 metres higher, when it comes to unpredictable drama, Stelvio is still the sport's absolute pinnacle.

It's also something of a gamble. Because of the Giro's springtime spot on the calendar, the unpredictability of the climate at such altitude makes the Stelvio's inclusion a risky proposition, which probably explains why it's been used rather sparingly. In total, it has appeared 10 times in the race, but had to be stricken from the route because of extreme weather in 1967, 1984, 1988 and 2013.

Precarious as it might be, however, it remains an integral

part of Giro history and cycling lore. As the Italians would say, *vale la pena* – it's worth the pain – because it rarely fails to produce drama. José Manuel Fuente courageously fought off the despotic Eddy Merckx here in 1972, and Bernard Hinault regained the Maglia Rosa from Wladimiro Panizza in 1980 with an impressive display of his own abilities and his team's superiority.

It has sometimes been the undoing of champions too, not least in 2005 when Ivan Basso fell foul to sickness and to the climb's unforgiving nature to lose a devastating 42 minutes and all hope of victory. After starting the 88th edition of the race as one of the favourites, the future two-time winner would eventually finish in Milan 27 places behind that year's victor, Paolo Savoldelli, all because of one bad day. And that's the charm. The Stelvio is more than a mountain, it's a protean monument of unpredictability, and whenever the race reaches its precipitous slopes, it treats spectators the world over to something that is all too rare these days: the simple pleasure of not being able to work out what will happen next.

8

GRACIOUS GIMONDI AND MERCILESS MERCKX

The *Gazzetta* called the 1976 Giro d'Italia 'The Miracle in Milan', a reference to Vittorio de Sica's classic neorealist fable of the same name. The race, too, had been a feel-good story with a happy ending. An ageing hero, past his prime, faces a peloton bursting at the seams with younger, hungrier talent, only to triumph in spite of it all.

It was Felice Gimondi's third Giro d'Italia victory, nine years after his first, the perfect swansong for an athlete who had reinvigorated Italian cycling and built a glittering palmarès of wins across the continent, from the cold cobbles of Roubaix to the promenade of Sanremo on the sunny Ligurian coast. He won the Tour de France in his debut season after his Salvarani team called him up as a late substitution. By his third year as a professional he'd become only the second man ever to win all three grand tours. In 1973 he became world champion and collected the second of his titles at the Giro di Lombardia, a race close to his heart and his home. Few riders before or since have won more, and yet for all that, Felice Gimondi is more famous for almost never winning.

Born to Mosè and Angela on 29 September 1942, the young Felice came into contact with cycling as a young boy and fell in love immediately. His father, a lorry driver who'd worked for 10 years in Brazil as a lumberjack, was a racing fan who used to take his son to see the greats of Italy's golden age compete whenever he could, but it was with his mother that he made his first tangible connection with the bicycle. The Gimondi family lived in Sedrina, a picturesque little town in the hills north of Bergamo, and Angela was its first postwoman. When she began riding a bike to complete her rounds more quickly, it caused a scandal because she was the first woman to do that, too. Shortly before her death in 2013 – she lived to be 103 – she joked with a journalist from the region's local paper, L'Eco di Bergamo, that it was so distressing for some of her neighbours that when the town's parish priest saw her passing, he'd rush out to scold her. Sometimes, her son would tag along.

The Gimondis were hard-working people, which served as a good base because later in life, Felice would have to labour incredibly hard for every victory. His first memory of bicycle racing was the 1954 Giro di Lombardia, close to his home, when Fausto Coppi won the event for the fifth time with an unassailable attack against Fiorenzo Magni. Growing up, Gimondi must have dreamed of being Coppi, but in the end, he had more in common with Magni. Blessed with talent and cursed by timing.

Once Felice started racing, it was clear that the boy had talent and he went on to an impressive amateur career, capped by victory at the 1964 Tour de l'Avenir, cycling's most prestigious race for up-and-coming talent. Even at that age, he was closer than he knew to his life's biggest obstacle. At the 1963 UCI Road World Championships, held in Renaix, Belgium, Gimondi finished a forgettable 12th, but he still remembers one key event in its lead up perfectly. Racing locally to prepare, he formed part of an attack of six riders, 90 kilometres from the finish. Slowly but surely, the group was whittled down, one by one, until the 21-year-old Italian was left alone with a local teenager. Close to the finish, Gimondi must have thought his victory a foregone conclusion, but suddenly his unknown companion found an extra gear, sprung his own assault and soloed to the line. Gimondi, one of Italy's great hopes, on the brink of what was surely going to be a prosperous professional career, had just been roundly beaten by an 18-year-old kid named Eddy.

Édouard Louis Joseph, baron Merckx – to give him his full name – was born three years later than Gimondi, on 17 June 1945 in Meensel-Kiezegem, around 50 kilometres west of Brussels, the Belgian capital. No one raced in his family, or indeed in his middle-class neighbourhood either. Cycling was, and still is in many parts, a working-class sport. But Eddy was smitten from the first time he threw his leg over a top tube and it was obvious to him that he had to race. In interviews, he has called it a vocation. Merckx grew up idolising Stan Ockers, the Belgian champion who won La Flèche Wallonne, Liège–Bastogne–Liège, the Tour's green jersey for the best sprinter and the World Championships in an incredible 1955 season, before dying in a crash the following year.

Like Gimondi, Merckx turned professional in 1965, but would take a little longer than the Italian to find his place in the sport. When he did, there would be little room left for anyone else. Between 1966 and 1976, he won Milano–Sanremo seven times. That alone would be enough to make him a legend, because only Costante Girardengo comes close, and Girardengo won his six titles when the sport was in its infancy and nowhere near as quick or competitive. Merckx also won each of the other four Monuments at least twice, retiring with a staggering 19 victories in cycling's five most important one-day races. That's eight more than his compatriot and rival on the cobbles, Roger De Vlaeminck, the original Monsieur Paris–Roubaix, and more than double the totals of luminaries like Coppi, Sean Kelly and Rik van Looy.

Between his debut and his retirement in 1978, Merckx won 525 races, a little less than a third of the events he entered. But more staggering still, that statistic is skewed by the final, fallow few years of his career, when the ravages of his voracious appetite for victory and his year-round racing schedule had caught up with him and sent him into sharp decline. At his peak, he won over 40 per cent of the races he started, racking up 54 victories in 1971 alone. To put that in context, by the end of 2016, three-time Tour de France champion Chris Froome had won 38 in his entire career.

Describing Merckx in 1972, Gianni Mura, inventive as ever, likened him to a force of nature that 'sweeps the plain and throws up waves over the dams, the strongest wind that there is, the most feared on earth and in the sea'. Which left poor Gimondi peddling into a gale. Merckx was stronger and greedier than anyone else and, when he was in form, success became almost inevitable. So much so that in racing circles, they'd joke that event organisers had to arrange two arrival times, one for Eddy and another for everyone else.

That was great if you were a fan of Merckx, and they were legion, but there was little to whet the appetite of the neutral or the romantic, yearning for the halcyon days of times past, when the cost of victory looked almost crippling and when even the preternatural talents had just enough troubles to remind everyone that they were, in spite of appearances, human. Eddy was the greatest since Coppi, perhaps the greatest ever, but in being so good he was bad to watch. People grew bored. And much like they'd done 40 years before, when Alfredo Binda was 'too good' for his own good, they started accusing Merckx of killing the Giro.

Writing in *La Stampa* during the 1973 Giro, Maurizio Cara-vella challenged that popular perspective, saying: 'Without Eddy's enterprises, cycling doesn't exist. That's the truth. Without him, the others seem like bewildered little boys, who don't know what to do. Merckx always wants to win, but that's not a defect.' He went on to cite the man himself, who could be as quick with an intelligent response as he was on the bike. 'What should I do?' asked a bewildered Merckx, 'stand aside and say to the others: "Welcome, make yourselves comfortable, pretend I'm not here"? Whoever doesn't give his best is the one who kills cycling. Maybe I would be smarter to hold back and give the race more suspense, but I'd be less honest.'

Gimondi, in that sense, had more appeal for the average Giro fan. It helped, of course, that he was Italian. He still holds the record for the most podium finishes at the Giro, nine in total: two second places and four third-place finishes to go with his three wins. It seems reasonable to think that without Merckx, more of those would have been on the top step. But Felice means 'happy' in Italian, and it suited him. He never griped when he lost or gloated when he won, a countenance perfectly suited to a rider that almost certainly would have been, in any other era, the protagonist. He was loved for his gregari-ous personality, respected for the dignified way in which he accepted his lot, and applauded for the resolve and intelligence that defined him as a racer, for the manner in which somehow, incredibly, he sometimes found a way to beat the unbeatable.

He didn't always do it by a hair's breadth, either, like his spiritual predecessor, Magni. He twice beat Merckx head to head in the Giro, finishing almost 12 minutes ahead of him in 1967 and almost eight minutes in front in 1976. Eddy was by that point past his best, but so was Felice, who was, after all, three years older. Gimondi's great strength lay in his patience and his alertness. He might not have been Merckx's equal in terms of talent but he could be close enough to take advantage in those rare moments when Merckx let down his guard. That era was full of talented stage racers – Luis Ocaña, José Manuel Fuente, and the 'Eternal Second' Raymond Poulidor – but Gimondi was the only one who could consistently stand up to Eddy on the big occasion. Sure, he would go four years, from 1968 to 1972, without directly beating Merckx at a single race, but he was close, and for many that was good enough.

Gimondi's Giro win in 1969 was a surprise to everyone, and a blight on Merckx's CV that he still contests. The Belgian was in a typically ruthless mood that May, winning four stages and building up a comfortable lead of a minute and 41 seconds over his Italian foil, with the Dolomites still to come. But after stage 16, a drug test revealed traces of Fencamfamine in Merckx's urine. The stimulant, used to fight fatigue and improve concentration, was rumoured to be popular in the peloton, but it had only recently been added to the list of banned substances. His B sample confirmed suspicions. Eddy Merckx, the Maglia Rosa, was out of the race. Upon hearing the news, the 24-year-old broke down in tears and desperately pleaded his innocence to the demented swarm of journalists that descended on his hotel. It was to no avail. The Belgian government sent the royal airplane to collect the nation's beleaguered hero and Gimondi was the new race leader. Elegant as ever, he started the stage in his normal team kit, and left the pink jersey in his suitcase for another day.

Later that year, at a track race in the French town of Blois, Merckx crashed when a power cut plunged the velodrome into darkness. The race was being paced by a derny, a motorised bicycle used to get track riders up to speed, and its driver, Fernand Wambst, died. Merckx cracked one of his vertebrae in the crash and afterwards maintained that he was never the same rider. He might not have been, but it made little or no difference to his results. The Belgian returned to the Giro the following May with a flawless classics campaign under his belt and a big point to prove. In exorcising the demons of 1969, he was pitiless, taking the Maglia Rosa after stage seven and never coming close to losing it. He skipped 1971 but reappeared in 1972 to dole out more misery, romping to victory by five-and-a-half minutes once the erratic Spaniard José-Manuel Fuente – a maestro in the mountains but lacking the consistency required to really excel – had exhausted himself in vain. The 56th edition, in 1973, was Peak Merckx: he won six stages and held the Maglia Rosa from start to finish, something that no one had managed since Alfredo Binda in 1927. By the finish in Trieste, Gimondi was the only rider less than 10 minutes behind him in the general classification.

Even for a rider like Merckx, though, what happened 12 months later was special. Just when it looked like Fuente had finally come to the Giro with enough to best Merckx – and Gimondi – he suffered one of the race's most dramatic ever collapses, forgetting to eat on stage 14 thereby allowing Eddy to chew up his slender lead. The Spaniard had been 18 seconds in front of Merckx that morning and six hours later he was eight minutes behind. The crack allowed a precocious talent by the name of Gianbattista Baronchelli into the dogfight and it was he, a few months shy of his 21st birthday, who would run Merckx the closest. Fuente fought back valiantly and finished the race with five stage wins, but it wasn't enough to make up for his error. It was tight – Merckx finished just 12 seconds ahead of Baronchelli and 33 ahead of Gimondi – but he had become only the third man to win the Giro five times. Later that summer, as if to underline his primacy after being so closely examined by Fuente and Baronchelli, he'd coast to victory at the Tour de France and cap off his year by winning the World Championships in Montreal. He was the first rider ever to hold the sport's three most important titles at the same time.

In those circumstances, Gimondi's final Giro in 1976 must have seemed like a dream. He was 33, and after enduring a decade of frustration peppered with just enough success to make it yet more frustrating, even he must have thought it past him. Merckx's star was fading, but Francesco Moser, Fausto Bertoglio and Johan De Muynck were all on the rise, eager to fill the vacuum left by the old guard's imminent departure. Moser was impressive in the early stages of the race, but found himself the victim of repeated, concerted attacks from his rivals, most notably the Brooklyn squad of Roger de Vlaeminck, Patrick Sercu and De Muynck. Unfortunately for the latter, the inevitable infighting that came with having a team full of race-winning talent meant that Brooklyn couldn't dominate the general classification battle to the extent that they should have. Sercu and De Vlaeminck were essentially competing against one another for stage wins and the race's points jersey, and De Vlaeminck was publicly furious with his young gregario, De Muynck, who had won stage six rather than waiting to help his team captain after a crash slowed him down. Had they spent less time squabbling among themselves, the Giro would have been De Muynck's because even without a team to support him he was the best rider in the mountains.

Gimondi held the pink jersey for the second week of the race, until stage 19's difficult trip to Torri del Vajolet, a route that involved six big climbs in the Dolomites. The Spanish gregario Andrés Gandarias won with a solo breakaway that day, but crucially, De Muynck finished almost 40 seconds ahead of his Italian rival, leapfrogging him in the general classification with a lead of 25 seconds. The next day's difficult climb over the unpaved and cruelly steep Passo Manghen would have been the perfect place for the in-form Belgian to seal his win, but when he asked his teammates for their support, they laughed in his face. He was alone. By contrast, two bad crashes that could have left Gimondi with huge time gaps were essentially cancelled out by the peloton, which chose both times to soft pedal until the popular Italian had rejoined the group. It pays to have friends in professional bike racing.

The penultimate stage finished in Bergamo, but a bad crash left De Muynck out of sorts and badly cut up. And as a *coup de grâce*, Gimondi snuck into the GC lead with victory, happily for him, on the day that finished in his home town. De Muynck's crash had drastic consequences, because on the final stage's TT, he was unable to hold the necessary position for the duration of the course due to his wounds, and he finished 44 seconds behind Gimondi, who won the overall Maglia Rosa by 19 seconds. Yet again, his stoicism and guile had paid off, and he took his third Giro without winning a stage until it really mattered. It was a masterclass in race management. Not Eddy's style, perhaps, but undoubtedly something he appreciated.

Neither ever begrudged the other victory, because they were never rivals, in the real sense. As racers, they existed in different worlds: Eddy was a god and Felice was matchless among the mortals. Gimondi would say that he regarded his real peer as his compatriot Gianni Motta, the 1966 Giro champion, and as for Merckx, well, Merckx was peerless. They were cordial competitors and remain good friends to this day.

Years after retiring, Merckx would call Gimondi his most loyal opponent, and despite the fact that he insists the Italian's World Championship victory was only possible because he was betrayed by his own Belgian team, he doesn't have a bad word to say about him. No one, not even Merckx, can win them all, and if you have to lose, it might as well be to a gentleman. There is, after all, a lot to admire in a man who had the most reason to be bitter about your success but chooses, instead, to be happy in his lot.

When the *Gazzetta* asked Gimondi in 2016 who he thought was the greatest ever sportsman, he replied warmly: 'Unfortunately, I have to say "Him", Eddy Merckx. Believe me, I knew him well; he put me through the pains of hell. He's the best because he was the protagonist in a sport at the highest level for an entire decade. He did everything, all year, every time with only one objective: To win. Classics, grand tours, climbs, sprints, road, track six days, even cyclocross. He even wanted to win the exhibition races. After that I'd say Muhammad Ali and Pelé, but they weren't like Eddy.' To which we might add there haven't been many like Felice, either.

BLOCKHAUS, ABRUZZO

It's 31 May 1967. Stage 12 of the 50th Giro. After seven hours in the saddle on a brutal 200-kilometre route that had already scaled three difficult peaks, the peloton encountered a new-comer to the race: the Blockhaus climb, in the thick of the Apennine Mountains. As the leaders approached the final kilo-metres, Italo Zilioli, a talented climber from Turin who had been second in the previous three Giri, surprised the Maglia Rosa José Pérez-Francés and the rest of his rivals with an attack. But he wasn't alone. There was another Giro debutant stuck on his wheel.

It seems incredible now, but at that point it wasn't clear that Eddy Merckx was a man for the mountains. Still two weeks shy of his 22nd birthday, the Belgian was riding in his first grand tour, having come to the Giro with a big reputation in the classics. He could sprint and he could certainly climb, and in one-day events he had the potential to win in any conditions, from one end of the year to the other, but no one knew whether he could consistently deliver over the course of a three-week race.

Merckx had held his own until stage 11, and was just over a minute behind in the general classification, tied a respectable seventh with Gianni Motta, and ahead of the 1965 champion, Felice Gimondi. But they hadn't seen anything yet. Eddy was about to give everyone a glimpse of just how good he really was.

The high mountains were uncharted territory for a rookie from the Low Countries, but he felt good, so he chased. Then, with a kilometre to go, he scorched past Zilioli to his first grand tour stage win, beating the Italian by 10 seconds and leaving Pérez-Francés and the waning Jacques Anquetil scrambling to limit their losses. Both Blockhaus and the Belgian had made an impression.

Twelve months later, the race returned. The little-known Franco Bodrero was the first over the line, but he soon saw his victory annulled when he was disqualified as part of one of the race's earliest doping scandals. Merckx had been unable to give the crowds an encore of his fireworks from the year before, but he didn't have to. He was already in pink, five minutes ahead of everyone, and only a day away from the first of his five Giro titles.

Blockhaus has only featured four times since then, and has not always been remembered for the right reasons. With hindsight, Ivan Basso's frighteningly quick ascent in 2006 cannot be mentioned without bearing in mind that shortly afterwards, the infamous Operación Puerto legal case in Spain would reveal the Italian's connections to the now-disgraced doctor, Eufemiano Fuentes. Basso won that Giro by almost nine and a half minutes, the biggest margin of victory since 1965. In the words of two-time Giro winner Gilberto Simoni: 'I've never seen anyone dominate like him; never seen anyone that strong. He seems like an extra-terrestrial.' Three years later, the stage was won by Franco Pellizotti, who, after a lengthy legal battle, had his 2009 results annulled by the UCI due to 'irregular blood values' in the build up to the 2009 Tour de France.

Its recently chequered past and infrequent usage notwithstanding, Blockhaus remains one of the Giro's iconic climbs and the toughest to be found south of the Alps and the Dolomites. There are three possible roads to the top. The least favoured by climbing connoisseurs begins in Fara Filiorum Petri, to the northeast, and is generally considered the easiest, with a lengthy approach averaging 6.5 per cent up to the Passo Lanciano and on to Blockhaus proper. Of the two routes from the northwest, Roccamorice and Lettomanopelo, the latter also passes through the Lanciano but has a tougher average gradient of more than 7 per cent, while the former takes a more testing approach, with sections tipping over 10 per cent. All three converge at the unmistakable Hotel Mamma Rosa, an imposing old boarding house decorated in flaking pink paint, for the final serpentine kilometres leading to the exposed and barren summit.

The surrounding Maiella Massif is an enchanting part of the country, a home to bears, wolves and wild cats and saturated with local legend. The actual Blockhaus, a military fortification from which the climb derives its name, was built shortly after the unification of Italy to combat gangs of native bandits that resisted the central power of Italy's newly formed government and operated from secluded bases, scattered across the mountainside. One of the climb's unique features is a huge stone, known as the *Tavola dei Briganti*, which is inscribed with details of the outlaws' daily lives, and with statements of defiance. 'This was a kingdom of flowers,' says one, before adding, 'Now it is a kingdom of misery.'

9

THE SHERIFF AND THE RIFLE SHOT

Francesco Moser and Giuseppe Saronni are like l'acqua e il fuoco, water and fire. If one said snow was white, before he had a chance to finish his sentence the other would be shaking his head and furiously declaring that it was black as the night. That's assuming, of course, that you could get them to agree to be in the same room together in the first place. Because even now, three decades after they last raced one another, the animosity continues, and you get the sense that they derive a unique and perverse pleasure from taking shots at one another. To many tifosi, their rivalry epitomised an important divide in Italy's society. Moser, the perfect expression of the country's gritty, agrarian backwaters; Saronni, a son of Lombardy's wealthy industrial heartland.

Francesco was born in 1951 in Palù di Giovo, a small town that overlooks Trento in the foothills of the Dolomites. One of 11 children, as a boy he'd accompany his father to watch the Giro whenever it passed, and grew up steeped in cycling culture because not one, not two, but three of his older brothers, Diego, Aldo and Enzo, were professionals. Aldo and Enzo both wore the Maglia Rosa for two days in their careers, the former in 1958 and again in 1971, and the latter in 1964. This area is the kind of place that lives and breathes cycling, and more recently it has given us Gilberto Simoni, Giro champion in 2001 and 2003, and Diego's son Moreno, winner of the 2013 edition of the Strade Bianche. They're a tough, competitive family, and while Enzo died in a farming accident aged 67, Aldo, now in his eighties, can still be found tending to the grapes in the vineyards of the family estate. In 1973, the year Francesco made his debut as a professional, all four where involved with the Filotex team: three as riders and Enzo as a directeur sportif. Aldo was 39, some 18 years older than the fresh-faced Francesco. His first bike, aged five, was a gift from Aldo, and after that, in the great tradition of so many siblings, it was hand-me-downs. Some were so big that he'd ride them sitting on the top tube, up and down the steep, seven-kilometre stretch to the schoolhouse, rain or shine. Moser started racing relatively late, aged 18, because of familial duty in the fields, but when he won the Trentino Regional Championships in July 1969, there was no looking back. Equipped with a motor that was as powerful as his pedalling stroke was elegant, *Lo sceriffo*, the Sheriff, as he'd come to be known, embarked on a professional career that would culminate with an incredible 273 wins, including three Paris–Roubaix titles, victory at Milano–Sanremo and the World Championships, and two wins at the Giro di Lombardia, not to mention countless other one-day road races and a slew of track events. He also won the 1984 Giro d'Italia, the same year that he set a new Hour Record. In celebration of that achievement, his vineyard produces a sparkling wine called 51,151, the number of metres covered at the Agustín Melgar Olympic Velodrome in Mexico City.

Saronni discovered an aptitude for racing much earlier. Born in Novara but raised in Buscate, on the outskirts of Milan, his first bike was bought from Felice Branca, once a mechanic for Learco Guerra and Charly Gaul. He made the podium in his first race, at the 1970 Giochi della gioventù, a youth athletics competition organised by the Italian Olympic Committee. He was 12. Destined for great things early on, Saronni was nicknamed Il Balìn, local dialect for 'The Baby'. As a teenager he raced on the road, cyclocross, and track, and as an 18-year-old, competed at the 1976 Olympics in Montreal as part of Italy's team pursuit squad. The following season he turned professional, with a special dispensation from the federation allowing him to do so before he turned 20. In his first outing as a pro, he finished second at the Trofeo Laigueglia in Liguria, hot on the wheel of the reigning world champion, Freddy Maertens. Five weeks later he took the first of 173 professional victories with full honours at the Trofeo Pantalica, what was then an important early-season race based around Syracuse in Sicily. Moser was third, and a rivalry was born. Somewhat ironically, the Sheriff still claims that he only lost that race after being blocked by a police motorcycle. He also claims to have knocked the driver off the road. Saronni, meanwhile, maintains that it wouldn't have mattered a jot. Moser was by that time an established champion, he'd worn the Tour's yellow jersey in 1975 and the Maglia Rosa at the 1976 Giro, where he also took the points classification with three stage wins. But it was obvious that he'd have to keep an eye on the newcomer.

The contrasts between the pair made for easy factionalism among the tifosi, too. For instance, in 1978, Moser won the first of three Paris–Roubaix titles, soloing home almost two minutes ahead of the great Belgian classics specialist, Roger De Vlaeminck, in a day characterised by brutal weather. Moser looked like a force of nature, more than a match for his adversaries and the elements, cutting a slice through the rain and gliding over the wicked cobbles of northern France, resplendent in the world champion's rainbow jersey. Saronni finished the day alone, miserable, and wrapped up in the back of a team car. Three years later, while Moser was celebrating his hat-trick of back-to-back wins, a feat that only one other rider, Octave Lapize, had managed since L'enfer du Nord began in 1896, Saronni was busy complaining to the press. Never one to mince his words, he told the inquisitive journalists that Paris–Roubaix was a glorified cyclocross race that had no business on the road calendar, something that did not endear him to race fans in northern Europe or the partisan Moser faithful back in his homeland. Saronni was a powerful sprinter and, in the right conditions, an effective race winner, as his palmarès would attest. But in the eyes of some, he was soft. Worse still, some accused him of being a wheel-sucker.

In a purely competitive sense, what was to come was nothing compared to the paradigm of Bartali and Coppi, but the pair's obvious antipathy towards one another captivated the collective consciousness of cycling fans up and down the peninsula. Abroad, it was seen as parochial and largely inconsequential, probably because neither rider had any interest in the Tour de France. But at home it sold a lot of newspapers because journalists could bet on getting a great quote from whoever lost – or from the pair of them whenever their squabbling allowed someone else to steal the win. To pick just one of many classic exchanges, a race report in the Corriere della Sera from March 1979 records a surprise victory for Giovanni Battaglin at the Trofeo Pantalica. With Moser and Saronni both happier to lose than risk the other winning, Battaglin slipped off and beat Moser's domestique Palmiro Masciarelli easily at the line. 'I had Masciarelli in front of me, why the hell should I damn myself to catch the leaders?' fumed Moser at the finish. 'There was nothing to do. I didn't pull because I had no reason to. Saronni didn't pull because he didn't want to favour me.

It's a terrible story that has to end.' Saronni saw it differently: 'As long as Moser refuses to quit riding this way, I won't win, but neither will he. When he decides to cop on, it will be a beautiful day.'

A few months after that disagreement, the two of them would go head to head at the 62nd edition of the Giro. Its 3,301-kilometre route was one of several from Vincenzo Torriani that had a markedly different character to classic Giri. Seven of the previous nine editions had gone to foreigners, and impartial observers noted with interest that the race director's new penchant for sprint stages, important time trials and generous time bonuses coincided neatly with the rising fortunes of two popular Italians who struggled in the mountains. Torriani first created a Moser-friendly route in 1977, only to see the Sheriff robbed by the Belgian Michel Pollentier, nowadays most famous for pulling out of the 1978 Tour in ignominy, while wearing the leader's jersey, after a doctor discovered a condom filled with urine concealed under his armpit during a doping test. The following year was won by the Belgian Johan de Muynck, who mounted a surprise attack on stage three while the favourites marked one another, and then held on to his slender lead for the remaining three weeks. Moser was third, and Saronni, in his Giro debut, a credible fifth, with three stage wins.

The following year, 1979, they would be helped by Torriani, who laid out a parcours that was the flattest in the modern era and included five time trials. Newcomers to the sport might find this somewhat distasteful, but all three of the grand tours have a long history of creating courses to favour certain champions and, for the sake of the sport's grass-roots popularity, it's often been politically and financially expedient to consider a certain competitor's strengths when plotting out the parcours. Indeed, when the route was announced that March, the

Turin daily *La Stampa* applauded Torriani for finally protecting Italy's champions, proclaiming in the headline that, 'This Giro is made to measure for Moser and Saronni', and pointing out that the Tour had been cut for Jacques Anquetil 'like a suit', and posing the question, 'If you have a champion, why not protect him?' No doubt plenty of the tifosi wholeheartedly agreed.

Saronni was in scintillating form that May, with a stage win at Tirreno–Adriatico and two stages and the overall classification at the Tour de Romandie to his name. Not to be outdone, Moser had won the prologue at Tirreno–Adriatico and been victorious at Gent–Wevelgem and Paris–Roubaix. The race began with a prologue in Florence, and Moser was the first man in pink. His young rival was just three seconds behind. The race steered south, with sprint finishes in Perugia and then Castel Gandolfo, a small town in the hills south of Rome famous for being home to the pope's summer residence, with neither rider able to shake the other. Stage three's 31-kilometre time trial from Caserta to Naples was long enough to allow Moser's superior skills against the clock to shine, but despite averaging almost 50 kph, he could only prise 26 seconds from the determined Saronni. The following day, a difficult if not exactly epic mountain stage on rolling roads to Potenza in Italy's deep south, saw the pair's main rival, two-time Tour champ Bernard Thévenet, inexplicably losing seven minutes to the stage winner, Claudio Bortolotto. Moser and Saronni, glued together, came in half a minute behind first place, with the difference in the general classification fixed stubbornly at 22 seconds. But something would have to give.

Stage eight provided a much-needed shake up. It was an uphill time trial, from Rimini on the Adriatic coast, to the microstate of San Marino, nestled in the Apennine Mountains, and Saronni used it to make a resounding statement. The

21-year-old rampaged home 32 seconds ahead of the towering, powerful Norwegian star Knut Knudsen in second. Moser, in fourth, was a shocking minute and 24 seconds off the pace, and out of the Maglia Rosa, 62 seconds adrift in the general classification, behind the young pretender to his throne. The gap increased on stage 10 to Portovenere, when another imperious TT from the man in the Maglia Rosa added 38 seconds to his lead. Ostensibly more of a bunch sprinter than a rider for long solo efforts, Saronni was beating Moser at his own game, and as the race finally headed for some high mountains, he was about to prove himself superior on the route's steeper slopes, too.

With a final 45-kilometre time trial to Milan planned for the last stage, the Giro was not yet beyond Moser, but his grasp on Saronni was starting to look tenuous. The younger of the two men had stolen another precious six seconds on stage 16 to Pieve di Cadore, and as the peloton prepared for the only rest day of that year's event, it was obvious that whoever was going to win the 1979 Giro would have to be perfect in the next two mountainous days as well as the closing TT. *Corriere della Sera* billed it as: 'I tre giorni della verità.' The three days of truth.

Stage 17 featured both the Falzarego and the Pordoi early on, but the two classic Dolomite climbs came well before the finish, which ended in a bunch sprint. Maybe he was the strongest that day, or perhaps none of his rivals wanted to vex him, but it was the home-town hero Moser who crossed the line first, to rapturous applause from his legions of fans in Trento. Prestige for the locals' favourite, then, but no profit: Saronni finished right behind him and kept his lead at a minute and 45 seconds. The following day's route tackled the Passo Tonale and the Passo dell'Aprica, but once again, their premature positioning on the parcours allowed the rouleurs to catch the climbers well before the stage's business end. Neither protagonist was at the very front that day, but Saronni did manage to purloin more valuable time on Moser, albeit just three seconds separating the two after 250 kilometres and the final climb to the finish in Barzio. There was no hope for the Sheriff. At his best, he was certainly capable of overturning a deficit of less than two minutes in a 45-kilometre time trial – he'd beaten Il Balin by two minutes and 12 seconds at the previous year's Giro over the same distance – but by the end of the 62nd Giro, after a long classics campaign in the spring, he was some way from his finest form. And Saronni was in irresistible shape. He romped home to another stage win, his fourth of the Giro, beating a young Roberto Visentini by 15 seconds and Moser by six more. That last victory meant that he beat Moser 275 to 257 in the points competition but, more importantly, with a cushion of two minutes and nine seconds, the Maglia Rosa was his, making him the race's youngest champion since Fausto Coppi.

Not content with dominance in the Tour and the Vuelta a España, Bernard Hinault joined the party in 1980. So too did Giovanni Battaglin, who had missed 1979 when his half of the Inoxpran squad came down with conjunctivitis. Wladimiro Panizza, a loyal gregario to Felice Gimondi turned grand tour rider in his own right, was also among the favourites, in what looked, on paper, to be an intriguing Giro. The 22 stages covered 4,025 kilometres, several mountain-top finishes and – not counting the short opening prologue in Genoa that didn't count towards the general classification – almost 90 kilometres of time trialling. It was a route that favoured the most complete athlete: it wouldn't be enough to distance rivals in the mountains, or a safe bet to annihilate them in the time trial. The winner was going to have to be good for three weeks straight. The big names all came with big results. Hinault, the most dominant rider of the age, was hot from victory at the Tour de Romandie and a Herculean performance at that spring's Liège–Bastogne–Liège. In what was arguably the most dramatic edition of the sport's oldest Monument, only 21 of the 174 starters finished, and the *Le Blaireau*, French for The Badger, crossed the line with almost 10 minutes' advantage over second place – and frostbite in two fingers that would cause lifelong damage. Moser, the reigning world champion, had been dominant at Tirreno–Adriatico and became the first man to win three editions of Paris–Roubaix consecutively. And Saronni? The first thing he did after triumphing at La Flèche Wallonne was to tell the huddled reporters: 'I have to thank Moser for this. His victory in Roubaix stimulated me.' Compliments don't come much more obviously backhanded than that.

Moser, as was his wont, won the opening prologue ahead of Knut Knudsen and Hinault, but no one could match Saronni in the opening three road stages. All three finished in bunch sprints, and all three went to the previous year's winner, still only 22, and seemingly getting better with each passing season. The Sheriff and the Badger were never far behind, however, and so Moser stayed in pink until stage five, when a wet time trial to Pisa surprised everyone, first because it was won by the relatively unknown Jørgen Marcussen, at the Giro in support of Battaglin, and second because the runner-up, Hinault, managed to put a minute into Moser and almost two into the obviously exhausted Saronni. The Frenchman looked like having the Giro sewn up already, until a breakaway on Tuscany's tallest mountain, Monte Amiata, saw a group slip away while the three big favourites all marked one another. That bunch included the day's winner, Silvano Contini, but crucially it also included Roberto Visentini, who had started the day fifth in the GC, a minute and 20 seconds behind Hinault, only to finish it two minutes and 58 seconds ahead of the Frenchman in the overall standings. With such a commanding lead over the sport's pre-eminent rider, there was some talk of an Italian coalition to keep Hinault away from the podium but, given the antipathy between Moser and Saronni, that was never likely. And so, with the home contingent divided, the Badger kept his head down, and bided his time. Beppe Saronni got back to winning ways on stage 13, coming first in a sprint finish in Barletta, on the peninsula's southern Adriatic coast. By then, however, he was out of the running in the GC. Moser lay in 10th, almost four minutes off the pace, and Hinault in seventh, just two seconds shy of three minutes behind Visentini. But 24 hours later, it would be a different story.

Hinault's attack on stage 14 showed just how good – and how vicious – the Badger could be. He laid waste to all but one rider, the aforementioned Panizza, on a gruelling day in the Apennines, finishing at the ski resort in Roccaraso. The Renault team's gambit was to launch Hinault's strongest domestique, Jean-René Bernaudeau, in an early attack. Bernaudeau was making his debut at the Giro, but had obvious grand tour pedigree, having finished fifth at the 1979 Tour. In short, he was too good to let go alone, and so the peloton chased like dogs, while Bernaudeau's captain, ensconced comfortably in the bunch, got a free ride. The mountains that make up Italy's spine are not as imposing as the Alps or the Dolomites, but they can be brutally steep, and by the penultimate climb to Rionero Sannitico, deep into the interior on the border between Molise and Abruzzo, all but the most gifted of riders were scattered in Hinault's wake. Moser and Saronni fought bravely to hold on, but neither were climbers, and by the finish the Badger had distanced them comfortably. The young Visentini was as capricious and fragile as he was talented, and not for the last time in a career that promised so much he suffered a total mental and physical breakdown, losing more than six minutes. The 35-year-old Panizza, the man who still holds the record for the greatest number of appearances at the Giro, with 18 starts and 16 finishes, was the new race leader. He was from a family of communists, and had been named after Vladimir Lenin: a proud red, now in pink after toiling so long in the service of others.

The following days took the peloton north, along a flat parcours that kept the general classification fastened in a deadlock. Giovanni Battaglin moved himself into the podium places with a daring solo ride on stage 18 that caught everyone by surprise, but it was the stage two days later, from Cles to Sondrio, over the Passo delle Palade and up the north face of the Passo dello Stelvio, that would ultimately decide the 1980 Giro d'Italia. It had been planned perfectly by Renault's directeur sportif par excellence, Cyrille Guimard. As a rider he'd been a contemporary of Eddy Merckx, a match for anyone in the mountains on his day, but it was as a DS that he truly shone, and many believe him to be the best of all time. After the Palade, Guimard dispatched three of his riders, including Bernaudeau, as part of a break, which was foolishly let go by the Italians. Before the start of the Stelvio they led by more than six minutes and, although they were caught as soon as the gradient increased, Bernaudeau had escaped solo and was now waiting up the road for Hinault, who could taste blood. The Badger exploded from the bunch with an almost inconceivably aggressive lunge, leaving everyone but Battaglin, Panizza and Bianchi's Tommy Prim for dust. Once the four were free, there was another attack from Hinault. This time, he was too much for Prim and Battaglin, but Panizza, still in the Maglia Rosa and no doubt aware that this would be the defining moment of an otherwise modest career, clung on for dear life, and for posterity. But he could only do so much, and his sober talents were no match for the superhuman Hinault, at the zenith of his powers and determined to win the Giro. One more kick, and he was gone, winding his way up Italy's most famous climb alone, in search of his loyal lieutenant and what now was certain victory. Unusually for a Stelvio stage, the finish was still almost 90 kilometres away, but the French duo put on a masterclass in team time trialling and hammered away incessantly until they reached Sondrio, almost five minutes ahead of the chasing pack. For Bernaudeau, there was the reward of a prestigious stage win; and for his captain, a place in the record books. With a lead of more than three minutes in the general classification, the penultimate day's 50-kilometre TT was a mere formality: Hinault was the equal of anyone against the clock, and it mattered little to him that Saronni took his seventh stage win. The following day in Milan, Le Blaireau from Yffiniac in Brittany became only the second Frenchman, after Jacques Anquetil, to win the Giro. He was, too, only the fourth to have won all three grand tours, and the first to do so at his first attempt.

Moser pulled out of the 1980 Giro quietly, with three stages to go, citing fever. And he didn't fair much better the following year, finishing more than half an hour behind the winner, Giovanni Battaglin, who triumphed in spite of another course seemingly tailored to everyone's favourite duelling duo. Torriani had constructed a parcours that favoured time trials and sprint stage wins, and though there were some difficult mountains, it was obvious to everyone just who was expected to benefit from the generous bonuses awarded to the top-placed finishers on each stage. So eager were the organisers to please Moser and Saronni, that when a scrap broke out between the two after the judges couldn't decide whether the Trentino star had finished second or third behind Saronni on stage five, they shared the GC podium until things calmed down. The time bonuses were such that the difference would affect whether Moser or Saronni was in pink, and so, with the press and the cameras of Italy's national broadcaster watching, both were awarded a pink jersey while the race commissaires made up their minds. Eventually, Moser was given the benefit of the doubt and the overnight lead, but he had to hand it over to his rival the next day, when Saronni took another stage win and, with it, more precious bonus time. At that early stage of the race, Torriani's convenient gratuities were adding up, rewarding Saronni to the tune of 90 seconds – had it been based purely on time elapsed, the 1979 Giro champion would have sat in a far more humble ninth position overall, regardless of his three stage wins. Pity poor Battaglin, having to compete with that. There was such anxiety about bias in favour of Moser and Saronni, in fact, that Davide Boifava, the Inoxpran directeur sportif, was afraid of outright cheating in the final time trial to Verona and threatened to follow Saronni with a video camera to make sure that he played by the rules and received no helping hands.

Hinault was back across the Alps, hungry as ever, to take his second Giro title in 1982. Neither Moser nor Saronni made the top five, but while Moser had a relatively quiet season by his standards, Saronni, now in his mid-20s, was prolific, taking the Tour de Suisse, Tirreno–Adriatico, the Giro del Trentino, Milano–Torino, and the Giro di Lombardia. He also donned the famous rainbow jersey that September in Goodwood, England, in what was one of the most famous World Championships in the modern era. Saronni won that day with a breathtaking sprint against two of the world's best riders, America's Greg LeMond and Ireland's Sean Kelly. So impressive was his final burst that it earned him the nickname 'The Goodwood Rifle Shot'.

Saronni, for a time, could do no wrong, and started the following year with success at Milano–Sanremo. For the 1983 edition of the Giro, the flat course favouritism and lavish time bonuses were present as ever in the 3,920-kilometre route, with only one of the 22 stages a genuinely difficult, mountainous test. The unpredictable Roberto Visentini, so often Saronni's sparring partner in their amateur days, was an accomplished time trialist, too, and so could not be discounted, but it was Beppe and Francesco who were expected to dominate. As it turned out, the usually imperious Moser, turning 32 a couple of weeks after the Giro's finish, was out of sorts and out of contention. For the whole season, in fact, he won almost nothing. Having been so commanding against the clock, it seemed as if time was finally getting its own back. Saronni raced to victory in the fastest Giro ever. No one could match him in the sprints, and in the mountains he consistently held his own. There were rumours – and some vocal protest from within the peloton – that his preferential treatment from the organisers was allowed to go so far that a blind eye was turned when he jumped the start in a time trial, but that was probably borne out of resentment rather than any hard evidence. Visentini, ever wronged, was among the protesters, bemoaning too the fact that his total elapsed time had been less than that of the winner.

Before retiring from that race, Moser made a point of congratulating his adversary. It looks like a final act of conciliatory benevolence from a man, seven years his senior, who Saronni had, in a perverse way, always admired, when all was said and done. He used to say that beating the Sheriff meant more than race victories, and as his old foe revealed to him that he was going to retire that season, it looked as if Saronni, twice champion, had got the better of him in their Giro grudge. Beppe admitted to being moved by the gesture, which must have made Moser's renaissance six months later all the more infuriating.

In January 1984, Francesco set a new Hour Record in Mexico City. Twice. His first effort bested Merckx's 1972 distance by almost a kilometre and a half, and a few days later he added another 300 metres for good measure. Embracing aerodynamic developments, he used disc wheels and a dramatically squat bike that tucked the rider low over the front wheel, cutting through the air like a rapier. With the help of Francesco Conconi, a pioneer in the field of sports science from the University of Ferrara, Moser was a rider reborn. The Hour Record was followed by victory at Milano–Sanremo, a race that had been an agonising absence on his palmarès. The 67th Giro d'Italia couldn't come soon enough.

Hoping for one last showdown between Saronni and the Sheriff, Torriani laid out a flat parcours, including a whopping 140 kilometres of individual time trials as well as a 60-kilometre team event, in order to favour his two compatriots over the rising star of French cycling, Laurent Fignon, who was debuting in the Giro with the Renault team, having won the Tour at his first attempt the previous summer. His failure to repeat the feat in Italy has been the subject of Italo-Franco tension among race fans ever since. Griping about the organiser's prerogative to design routes as he sees fit is a pointless enterprise because, as has been mentioned, they all do it. The Dolomite stages weren't quite taxing enough to allow the Renault rider to land a lethal blow, but c'est la vie. Fignon, however, maintained that Torriani's nepotism went much further. As the race entered the mountains, Moser was in pink but there was still an opportunity for Visentini and Fignon to take control, because there was still the not inconsequential matter of the Passo dello Stelvio on stage 18. The day before, however, panic had set in for the climbers as rumours spread. The pass was blocked with snow, and Torriani was going to cut it from the stage. The Giro director himself claimed that he wanted it to go ahead, but that the region's road workers, whose job it would be to clear the snow, had said it was impossible. The French magazine Vélo infamously disagreed, publishing pictures of the pass clear of snow and open to the public. Whatever the truth may have been, for the Giro's purposes it was abandoned, so instead, the peloton climbed the more sedate Tonale and Palade climbs and Moser was able to finish just five seconds behind the day's winner, Bruno Leali. Visentini, a teammate of Leali at Carrera, retired from the race in disgust and later claimed to have crushed his bike in a vice before sending it to Davide Boifava, his director, in a bin bag. Cyrille Guimard, now in charge of Fignon, was outraged too, claiming that fans had pushed Moser up the climb and had been allowed to draft team cars without punishment, while his own rider was penalised for taking food from support staff outside the designated feed zone. With more mountains to come, Fignon kept fighting, and narrowed the lead, but just couldn't shake Italy's grizzled champion, snug in the Maglia Rosa and entrenched in the group every day. With a little over a minute separating the pair, stage 20 was a wildcard. It was a loop of the Campolongo, Pordoi, Sella and Gardena climbs in the Dolomites in Alta Badia, but the up-and-down nature of such a circuit suited Fignon, the climber. In theory, however, it also gave Moser, famous for his descending skills, almost as much to be happy about. In the end, a gutsy move on the Pordoi left everyone flat-footed, and the Frenchman arrived at the finish in Arabba two minutes and 19 seconds ahead of the race leader. He kept the Maglia Rosa the following day, too, but on the final day's racing, a 42-kilometre time trial that finished in Verona, Moser had the last word.

Tens of thousands lined the roads to see the defining moment of a career that had captured the country's imagination for the best part of a decade. Downtown Verona was heaving with fans, as their champion shot through the city's main square, Piazza Bra, and into its iconic Roman amphitheatre, emerging from the shadows of its arches to cross the line, exhausted. It was a bewildering display – just shy of 51 kph on open roads, faster even than his first attempt at the Hour Record, which had been on a track, at altitude. There were still several minutes to wait, but as the screams and songs of delirious tifosi filled the air with an atmosphere reminiscent of a heated football stadium, the writing was on the wall for Fignon. No one was going to better that. 'It was something that I wasn't expecting,' said Moser, after the podium, 'and something that few people still believed could happen.' As the dust settled, there were those who still refused to believe it could happen, either. Because while in Italy it was seen as a romantic, resounding victory for an almost universally loved rider at the end of his career, abroad, the polemics continued. The French press cried foul play in the mountains, and for the rest of his life, Fignon would maintain that the RAI television helicopter had ridden behind Moser so as to push him along, but above the Frenchman, to bury him beneath its downdraft. In Moser's defence, however, the arguments against him conveniently forget to mention the fact that had Fignon – still only 23 and not yet the finished article – not imploded on stage five's climb to the Blockhaus in Abruzzo, the result would have been very different. Fignon's attack that day had looked like a thing of beauty, but turned out to be youthful folly, when, suffering from hunger, he broke down before the summit and in the space of a few kilometres lost almost a minute and a half to Moser. This, from a rider who would beat the great Hinault by more than 10 minutes a month later at the Tour. With a cooler head, the Giro would have been his regardless of the Stelvio or the dubious helicopter conspiracy.

Moser had his Giro. It was the end of his career, though, part swansong from a fading hero, part offering from the organisation in honour of a champion and his battalion of tifosi. Saronni, who turned 27 that year and with two Giri victories already under his belt, should have had enough left in him to play a leading role into the next decade, but after his win in 1983, it was as if an incredible hunger had been permanently sated. Or rather, in the eyes of many fans, as if, while not having lost his appetite for victory, over time, the work and the sacrifice involved had become unpalatable. He enjoyed the off-season, and the fame, and from the outside at least, seemed to possess little of the obstinate, proletarian work ethic that drove riders like Hinault or Moser. His career limped on for another seven years, until at the 1990 Milano–Torino, the bells tolled, some two seasons after a champagne cork had last popped in his honour. It would be callous, and more than a little disingenuous, to say that a racer with almost 200 victories to his name never fulfilled his true potential, but it must have been a sad thing to watch his talents peter out slowly. Getting dropped on descents, without a decent win in years, was no way for a two-time Giro champion to leave the stage.

At the height of his abilities, Il Balin had been Italy's best hope against Le Blaireau, but there was no question that Hinault was the better rider. Aside from his five Tours de France and two victories at the Vuelta, the Frenchman had a perfect record at the Giro: three starts and three wins. The pair didn't get along too well, either, and Hinault was an unapologetic *Moserista*. Speaking in 1983 to the late Italian journalist Fulvio Astori, who told him that Saronni, cocky as ever, thought that the Frenchman disliked him because it was so hard for him to win races compared to the Italian, who simply had to wait for a sprint, the patron of the peloton responded simply: 'And who beat him in a sprint at La Flèche Wallonne? Hinault, I think. I also think that Hinault is quicker than him in the mountains. Moser is more likeable, more approachable and more open. If he needs anything, my door is always open, and whenever I've needed anything, I've been his guest in Palù. It would be nice to have the same relationship with Saronni, but he's a lot more difficult. It's not that I have anything against him, he just has a certain type of character ...'

Perhaps without Moser, Saronni lacked inspiration. The pair had vexed one another for 10 months of the year, every year, and it must have been something to know that the fans, the press, the country, was both divided and delighted by the polar opposition. Unlike so many sporting rivalries before and since, it had been sincere and true to life, on and off the bike. It was a clash of backgrounds, styles and characters, a fundamental incompatibility.

They raced together, once, in a two-man time trial called the Trofeo Baracchi, in 1979. They couldn't even bring themselves to warm up at the same time, and met just before the start instead. Seeing the funny side of it now, Saronni jokes that Moser dragged him around the course at an inhuman speed on purpose, that he couldn't sit down afterwards, that he was destroyed, and that his teammate would have preferred to cross the line alone, and lose. Moser jokes that Saronni was so small, even when he pulled on the front, that it was Moser who took the wind.

It was a duality that stimulated them both, and while Moser and Saronni couldn't stand one another's company, it was a conflict ultimately based on mutual esteem. Both riders would have been far too proud to enter into a feud with anyone they thought little of. Saronni, the efficient finisher, grew up in awe of the older rider's spirit, the force of will and determination that he translated into dashing attacks and dramatic victories. Moser, the expressive soloist, must have envied Saronni's speed, his youth, and the fact that the wins seemed to come so much more easily to him. If they'd spent less time fighting one another and more time racing, both would have almost certainly won more, but where's the fun in that? Their enmity is a gift that keeps on giving, even as the one they used to call The Baby approaches his 60th birthday. When the *Gazzetta dello Sport*'s eloquent correspondent Marco Pastonesi caught up with them both, separately of course, in 2015, Moser was still kicking up a fuss about the time that Saronni had been so bold as to boast that he could beat him in slippers. Pastonesi relayed the offence to Saronni, who countered, sharp as ever: 'I didn't say slippers. I said tennis shoes.'

TRE CIME DI LAVAREDO, VENETO

If at first you don't succeed, try again. That was the attitude of the legendary race director, Vincenzo Torriani, when the spectacle he had planned for the 1967 Giro descended into farce. The Tre Cime di Lavaredo was the latest in a string of crippling, glorious climbs that Torriani had introduced to the Corsa Rosa since taking over from Armando Cougnet in 1949, but it didn't have quite the impact he'd hoped for on its debut. Crowds of fans pushed the riders up the brutal final kilometres, wiping out the lead by Wladimiro Panizza, who found himself overtaken by a hoard of lesser riders near the peak. Immediately after the finish, the day's winner, Felice Gimondi, declared it a 'disgrace'. The next day's *Gazzetta* continued the reproofs with a front page that cried: 'The mountains of dishonour.'

Undeterred by the fiasco, Torriani made sure that the Tre Cime returned the following May, as the grand finale to stage 12's 213-kilometre route from Gorizia, on the Yugoslavian border. Just as they had been in 1967, the conditions were woeful, the peaks veiled in thick storm clouds as the riders suffered through snow and heavy winds. But the fans controlled themselves and left the peloton to suffer honestly on what remains one of Italy's most difficult ascents.

Starting on the banks of Lake Misurina, deep in the Dolomites, it's a 7.5 kilometre slog to the Rifugio Auronzo at the top, where the altitude reaches 2,320 metres. Taken as a whole, the gradient averages a testing enough 7.5 per cent, but it's the final four kilometres that do the real damage, where the pitch rarely dips below 11 per cent and in parts ramps up to an excruciating 19 per cent. All of which made it the perfect stage for what Eddy Merckx still believes was his greatest performance.

The Belgian did a number of incredible things at the Giro, including holding the Maglia Rosa from stage one until the finish in 1973, but no day epitomises his supremacy quite like Tre Cime in 1968. Having announced his arrival on Blockhaus the previous spring, the 22-year-old was now considered a top contender for the general classification in any race he entered, but after 11 stages of the 51st Giro, he was still a minute and a half behind Michele Dancelli, a courageous, punchy rider who was famous for being among the most consistent winners of his generation, and for the lengthy, lone breakaways that he liked to undertake. In reference to that racing style, the great Gianni Mura once called him, 'Un sognatore nomade', a nomadic dreamer.

Early in the day, the leading contenders allowed a group of 12 optimistic riders to escape up the road, and as the weather worsened, their lead grew to more than nine minutes. Merckx, having been dropped when a mechanical issue forced a bike change, chased like a rabid dog, through sheets of sleet and violent squalls, dragging his gregario Vittorio Adorni back up to Gimondi, Italo Zilioli and Gianni Motta and then past them, closing on the hapless leaders, oblivious to the cold despite his short sleeves, intent on a victory that would have seemed impossible to anyone else. By the top, Merckx had humbled the mountain and all but humiliated his rivals. None of the GC favourites could get anywhere close to him, and Gimondi finished six minutes back, in tears. Such was the force of his performance that he now led Dancelli by more than five minutes, relegating the erstwhile GC leader to third by hauling Adorni up the mountain behind him. There were still 10 more stages in that year's Giro, but it was over. Merckx finished in Naples with four stage wins, the Maglia Rosa, and the jerseys for best sprinter and best climber, while his Faema squad took best team. The era of Merckx as the Cannibal had begun, and for the next six years, everyone else would be making do with leftovers.

10

ENTER THE AMERICANS

In the Giro in the early 1980s, foreign was a fairly relative term. It meant French, or maybe Belgian or Swiss, with the odd Spaniard to challenge in the mountains. Aside from the two wins by Luxembourg's Charly Gaul in the 1950s and the success of Swede Gösta Pettersson in 1971, Italy's biggest sporting prize was always shared among the sport's established superpowers. The 68th edition of the Corsa Rosa changed all that. Sure, Bernard Hinault still won ahead of Francesco Moser, but a group of upstarts from the US made the established order sit up and pay attention.

One star who was already clearly on the rise was Hinault's teammate, Greg LeMond, who made the podium aged 24. Grand tour trophies seemed a certainty for the Californian. What was far less certain was the effect that the race's sole American team would have on proceedings. 7-Eleven, an international chain of convenience stores, came into cycling as a sponsor in order to be involved in the 1984 LA Olympics and had no experience or knowledge of the sport. The Tour de France made sense because it was on American TV, but the Giro, all the way over in Italy, seemed a little bit pointless. The company had no commercial interests in the country and only diehard American cycling fans knew that the race existed. Nevertheless, once a local co-sponsor, Erminio Dell'Oglio of the Hoonved washing machine company, was signed up to help shoulder the financial burden, a band of enthusiastic riders were sent to the Bel Paese to pit themselves against the best in the world. Among them was a kid from the Midwest with big dreams and a very limited window of opportunity.

'I think we upset the apple cart,' says Andy Hampsten, laughing, as he recalls his first foray into grand tour racing, having been brought to the Giro by 7-Eleven on a one-month contract.

'We were almost all neo-pros, and we were supposed to genuflect in front of the big riders. I'm not going to say it was overwhelming – maybe it was in some ways – but I was very excited. This was something that I'd been working towards. I wanted to turn pro, and I was going to stop racing if I couldn't do it. After the US's Olympic successes, I knew there'd be quite a bit of interest in American riders and I needed to make it on to a pro team, one way or another. I was very focused on trying to get over to Europe.'

Like a lot of riders, Hampsten began cycling casually as a kid, but by the time he was 15, when his family moved to the UK, the bug had definitively bitten and not only was he racing seriously, but he was busy reading all about Europe's biggest races, and in particular the grand tours.

'When I was an amateur, I was fairly good at mountainous stage races,' he admits, almost reluctantly. Hampsten isn't one to boast, and whenever he discusses his successes, there's an eagerness to understate his obvious natural ability.

'I did well at the Coors Classic when I was 19 or 20, just before I turned pro, so I had my eye on big stage races, but never knowing when I'd do it. Then in 1985, I had an opportunity to turn pro – just for one month – with 7-Eleven, to round out their team for the Giro. I jumped at that occasion.

'I'd had quite a bit of experience racing in Italy as an amateur, there was a very good international programme for the American amateur team in the late 1970s and early 1980s, and I did some very good races there, the Settimana Bergamasca and the Giro della Regione. They were spring trips, so I'd go to France or to Italy. One year I won the prologue of the Settimana Bergamasca, which was a really important international amateur race at the time. So I'd had some success.

'I was fascinated by the cycling scene in Italy and I was so grateful to line up in Verona at the Giro in '85. It was a small team, I knew everyone very well, because they were mostly Americans that I'd raced with as an amateur. I was there as hired help, and there was no guarantee that I'd ever have another opportunity to come back, so I really wanted to do well. But I wasn't even sure if I was good enough.

'We didn't grow up in the system, if we failed there wasn't that support network, or the chance to go do the Vuelta or something, where people would say, "You were too young, try again next year." Those guys grew up with a foot in the door, we didn't even have a toenail in the door. That was common among not just the Americans, but all the English speakers and the Scandinavians.

'I knew that when top European pros came and raced the Coors Classic, I could beat them, because they had trouble with the altitude and they didn't know how fast Americans would go through corners in our crazy little criteriums. I was very comfortable on my own turf, and I'd raced in Europe so I knew I could beat them when they weren't on top of their game, but that didn't mean I could do it over in Italy at the Giro. I wasn't intimidated to the point where I didn't know what to do, but I was acutely aware of the fact that this was my one chance and that I couldn't waste it.'

No danger of that. Hampsten and the rest of 7-Eleven didn't know it at the Grande Partenza, but they were about to make history. But before that, they quickly started making waves. Now in his fifties, Andy divides his time between the US and Italy, where he runs a travel company catering to amateur cyclists, but at the time his understanding of Italian sporting culture was limited. They were expected to just make up the numbers and defer to the locals, but Hampsten and co. never got the message.

'It was an Italian race. I think even the French riders felt, if not intimidated, then not at home. It wasn't the international peloton of today where everyone's speaking English or some hybrid, we were in Italy, and the Italians wanted to race according to their traditions. None of us spoke Italian apart from Jock Boyer', full name Jonathan, aka Jacques and famous for being the first American to race the Tour de France. There's a pause, as Hampsten considers his words, before offering, with a chuckle: 'We rode like cowboys! When we were amateurs at something like the Settimana Bergamasca, with the Russians and the East Germans and the Czechs and Poles, we got to know them and to understand just how difficult it was for them even to get to the race, so when they'd have horrific crashes, you could understand it because it was so hard to get onto the team that crashing just wasn't a big deal for them. That was my experience. It was cowboy racing.

'There were a lot of crashes – the Italians need to wave their hands around when they talk and people did a lot of stupid things. My theory now, when I look back, was that we were a young team and it was a case of "blame the rookies". Not all of the crashes were our fault, but if there were one of us nearby we'd get blamed. And it was either a survival technique or horrible manners, but as amateurs we'd learned that whenever one of us was picked on, the rest of us would be ugly Americans and shout all the bad words that we'd learned that week. Not that anything ever happened – it's bike racing – but we were aggressive towards anyone picking on us.

'I saw it later in my career; the captains would break in the young riders by abusing them just because they'd been abused when they were rookies. We wanted nothing to do with that. We thought we understood that people were saying that the Americans were causing crashes because we were stupid or whatever, but the discussions were very brief – and obscene. It never came to blows or fists flying, but I think a lot of people were surprised at how little we were interested in being abused or initiated or whatever they thought they were doing.'

As 7-Eleven settled in, the rest of the race unfolded. The organisers had come up with a relatively balanced parcours, after coming under intense criticism in the preceding years for creating routes that obviously favoured the powerful, classics-specialist Francesco Moser, who'd won in 1984 and was the bookie's choice to take the pink jersey again in 1985. Laurent Fignon, who had won the previous two editions of the Tour de France, missed out due to an Achilles injury that ended his season after an impressive spring campaign, but his compatriot Hinault had crossed the Alps with his omnipotent La Vie Claire team looking to prove that he wasn't quite the spent force that many were making him out to be. Roberto Visentini, Marino Lejarreta, Johan van der Velde, Beppe Saronni and the aforementioned LeMond rounded out a star-studded peloton.

After Moser started stage one wearing pink thanks to a win in the opening prologue, he quickly lost it to his old rival Saronni in the team time trial on stage two. Hinault and Visentini showed their form once the race entered the mountains in stage four – and while Moser and Saronni were effectively out of contention by the finish-line that day atop the Val Gardena, the Giro's transatlantic newcomers were beginning to come to terms with their steep, grand tour learning curve.

'It was intimidating,' says Hampsten. 'I was very aware that I didn't have the skills, the talent, the experience. I appreciated the opportunity I had with the Giro d'Italia, but I was also acutely aware all the time that this was my one chance to get in. My first pro race was the prologue! And man, I wanted to be there. I knew that results was the only way I'd get onto a team, whether it was 7-Eleven or someone else, and I was just focused on doing well.

'I had an idea of my ability. I knew where I stood with the amateurs and I knew my style suited long, dragged-out mountain stage races. I had an inclination that the longer the race, the better. Not that I was ever the strongest, but my not incredibly generous talents as a bike racer suited very long, hard races because I recovered well. That didn't show up in many amateur races, but my stamina was good, it suited mountainous races, in the heat, and the more days there were, the better. And that's pro racing. So it didn't mean that I'd be a good pro, but I knew I could be a pro.

'That Giro was my big opportunity – and it didn't start well. The first day in the mountains, I blew up on the climb and lost a lot of time. So it wasn't that I was setting the Giro on fire from day one! The next few days after, it got to me. I went over it in my head, it was rainy, I hadn't eaten enough, I didn't have the stamina. It was empirical proof, I thought, "I'm not good enough."

'Though at the same time, I'm here, it's the Giro, it's fun. There was plenty of time to sulk, but I was hanging on, and as the race developed, everyone was getting more tired and having more problems, and I wasn't getting any worse. I wasn't getting dropped. My body was coming around. And the team was learning the whole time, we were improving as the race developed. And a grand tour is like heavyweight boxing – it's all about who's still standing in the final round. I might not have had a knockout punch, or the talent to ride away from everyone, but I was learning fast.'

It was plainer sailing for some of his teammates, and some early positives would end up inspiring much bigger achievements later on in the race.

'Our goal at 7-Eleven was to win one stage and to have a rider in the top 20. Mike Neel, the coach, was very good at managing us. He'd raced in Europe, and he knew we were skittish. But then in the first stage, a sprint, Davis Phinney was fourth. Three really good riders beat him, but we thought, "Oh my God, we didn't even plan that!" Only a couple of the team led him out, but when Davis went for it, he was fourth, even though we could have done a better job leading him out. It was fantastic. We weren't out of our league.

'At the first King of the Mountains climb, it was maybe a third category, not terribly tough, but whoever won it would have the jersey for a day, which would be cool. I sprinted for it, didn't get close, and just thought, "Bummer, that didn't work," but we turned off onto a small road, descending down, around 15 or 20 kilometres to the finish, and I'm eighth in line – with four world champions. It was incredible. I didn't get the KOM points, but I was on this descent with four world champions and it was surreal. One part of me was just thinking how unbelievable that was, but there was another voice telling me to do something, so I attacked. In the end, I didn't get close to winning; I got caught in the last 10 kilometres and I actually crashed in the field sprint. I crossed the line feeling like a complete fool, but Erminio Dall'Oglio, the co-sponsor, a wonderful man, came running over. I couldn't understand a word of Italian at that point, but he's hugging me, he's all over me.

And Mike Neel comes over and says "Andy, that was great." I thought, I didn't do anything near great, I got caught and then I fell over, but he said, "no, you're a pro now, you were on TV for 10 minutes! That's what the sponsors want. You went for it – that's all he wants." We just had to put on a show. That was the team spirit.'

The spirit elsewhere was less positive. As the Americans rode a wave of New World optimism, the traditional continental powers were involved in some traditional continental squabbles. Visentini, never one to shy away from confrontation or to underestimate his own abilities, was wearing the Maglia Rosa when he declared in a press conference that Hinault was past it and that if he won it was only thanks to his team's tactics and strength in depth. Shortly afterwards, the Badger put almost a minute into Moser and LeMond in a time trial down south, finishing one minute and 42 seconds ahead of Visentini, who had been duly humbled. That imperious performance gave Hinault the lead, more than a minute ahead of the Italian.

As the race returned north, it was 7-Eleven's time to shine. The veteran Ron Kiefel became the first American winner of a grand tour stage when he grabbed victory in stage 15 with a dramatic finish in Perugia.

'It was beautiful,' says a clearly nostalgic Hampsten. 'Ron Kiefel continually kept the 7-Eleven team going with his results. He'd won the Trofeo Laigueglia that February, which had really got the whole Giro ball rolling.

'That stage, I think it was a three-kilometre climb to the finish, was perfect for him. We were all working hard. But all the teams were up there, it was a nervous finish. There were definitely going to be time gaps and for the General Classification it was going to be an important day.

'I was up there to help Ron, I remember the finish being big wide boulevards and all the favourites were there. Lech

Piasecki, the great Polish time trialist was leading out Giuseppe Saronni for Del Tongo, Gerrie Knetemann, Francesco Moser, Bernard Hinault, they were all at the front. The lead-out trains were blowing up and Ron – it seemed like twice the speed of everyone else – just went streaking past. I don't know whether it was a kilometre or two, but there was still a bit to go, and the streets got narrower and there were cobbles, so we knew it would be hard for anyone to chase down an attack, but this was really far. He went sprinting away and held it. World champions going as hard as they could, and they didn't get anywhere near his wheel. It was absolutely incredible, one of the best victories I've ever seen.'

Their next trick was more of a shock for Hampsten, the rookie rider turned unlikely protagonist.

'Stage 19 was a huge day over big climbs, including the Cima Coppi. It would have been nice to win that because there was a special prize, but Mike Neel talked me out of trying anything.

'It was the last big day, I was 20th on GC and I wanted to move up. I wasn't a threat to the leaders, but there was a huge valley in the middle and if I tried to win and the peloton pulled to catch up, I couldn't hold them off. I was feeling really good and I wanted to show myself – but he convinced me not to and to put everything I had into the 58-kilometre stage the next day. It was a hard climb, not terribly steep, but a fairly long climb up a dead-end valley to the Gran Paradiso national park.

'I didn't like it. It was short, and I didn't think the peloton would be tired enough for me to get away. We rode it in the morning – the stage started after lunch – and I really didn't like it. There was a downhill in the middle, it wasn't steep enough, I couldn't see how I could wear everyone out so that I could sneak away.

'Mike told me: "You have to go early. Everyone knows you're climbing well but there are a lot of other riders hunting for a win. If you follow the regular script, you have no chance. You held back yesterday, so attack right at the beginning." So I did, I think I went in the first kilometre of the climb and I got away cleanly and held on.'

Here, Hampsten allows himself another self-deprecating laugh.

'I don't want to make it sound like a non-event. It was incredibly hard and I was wracked with doubts. I thought I'd gone too early, and people had been teasing me because I wore a one-piece, even though it was a normal road stage, and the team gave me a big lead-out to the base of the climb even though Hinault and Moser's teams were doing the same. But Mike had picked a corner where he thought I should go, to give me something to aim for, and right as another attack was getting absorbed by the peloton, it all bunched up on that bend, and just as the group fanned out across the road, I just squeezed out the front. I was pretty scared! It was all adrenaline, but there was so much pressure that I'd put on myself, accepting a plan that wasn't my idea, climbers like to attack when they see the whites of everyone else's eyes rolling back in their skulls, it was such a different way to approach a climb, but it worked – so well! We caught everyone by surprise.'

With two wins and a string of gutsy performances, the American underdogs on 7-Eleven had proven themselves worthy of a grand tour ride and Hampsten had proven himself deserving of a spot on the biggest team in cycling. His friend LeMond had urged his own bosses to watch his compatriot at the Giro and, when they liked what they saw, La Vie Claire duly signed the 23-year-old for 1986.

Elsewhere, Moser tried in vain to defend his title, allegedly with the help of the race director, Vincenzo Torriani, who casually cut a difficult climb from stage 19 to allow the Sheriff to claw back some time on Hinault. There were again accusations that the TV helicopter flew behind Moser to give him a push in the final time trial, but even that wasn't enough to deny the truculent Frenchman his third Giro win, making him the only foreigner ever to record a hat-trick of pink jerseys other than the peerless Eddy Merckx, who retired with five. Cycling was still a European show, but the Americans had proven that they were ready for their own share of the spotlight.

11

THE SAPPADA AFFAIR

When talking about conspiracy theories and election shocks, psychologists often point to something called Motivated Reasoning, a theory that proposes that humans, far from logical beings, are emotional beasts who are always looking to come to the conclusion that suits them best. Basically, it's confirmation bias on steroids, and when threatened by information that contradicts pre-existing loyalties or beliefs, sufferers ignore opposing opinions, regardless of the weight of evidence, in favour of protecting themselves by searching out information that appears to confirm their convictions. For examples of this, consider the people who think that the moon landings were a hoax, the diehard Elvis Presley enthusiasts who remain convinced that the King is alive and well, and almost any racing fan with an opinion about the 1987 Giro d'Italia.

Races don't get more dramatic than the 70th edition of the Giro, and even now, 30 years later, it still divides opinion among the tifosi in Italy. On paper, it looks straightforward: Stephen Roche comfortably beat Robert Millar by three minutes and 40 seconds, before going on to win that year's

Tour de France and World Championships, a Triple Crown of titles that had only been achieved once before, in 1974, by the inimitable Eddy Merckx. Roche's main rival in that year's Corsa Rosa, Roberto Visentini, didn't even reach the finish line, so to a casual observer it might seem like an odd thing to be debating so many years on. But, as always, the devil is in the details.

Visentini's 1986 Giro win had been a tour de force, and it launched the Italian to fame in his homeland. In a peloton packed with talent, he finished a minute and two seconds ahead of Giuseppe Saronni, and more than two minutes ahead of Moser. The sport's rising superstar, Greg LeMond, had been pipped to the podium by the wily old Italian, riding his final Giro, by just 12 seconds. The American had started among the favourites, and he would win the first of his three Tour de France titles a couple of months later, but a bad crash on stage two and a disappointing team time trial the following day had left the 25-year-old more than three minutes off the pace before the race had even finished its opening three days on the island of Sicily. Things could have been worse, however, and everyone was reminded of just how dangerous racing can be on the opening day, Monday 12 May. After a bad crash, medics deemed Atala's young Lombardian rider, Emilio Ravasio, fit to continue but after the finish in Sciacca, he fell into a coma and would die in a Palermo hospital two weeks later, just eight days before his 24th birthday.

The 69th edition was the last time that the race would be demonstrably tailored towards the ever-popular rivals Moser and Saronni, with Vincenzo Torriani, the race director, eschewing most of Italy's hardest mountains in favour of long flat stages, plenty of sprints and even more column inches as the quarrelsome duo went head to head one final time. In a country with as many spectacular mountains as Italy, it's hard to equitably defend the director's decision to distort the race's character just to suit two popular riders, but impartiality has never been a quality of cycling anyway, and to borrow an odd turn of phrase from the Italians, Torriani knew his chickens. Put simply, he was giving the public what they wanted.

When the gradient did increase, LeMond was never far from the front, chipping away at his deficit, while Saronni looked like a rider reborn, grabbing the Maglia Rosa early on in stage three and holding it for 10 days from stage six. He might have held it to the end had it not been for LeMond, who openly berated the race organisation for suggesting that stage 16 should be cancelled due to bad weather. Coincidentally, it also happened to include some tough climbs, which obviously didn't suit the man in pink. There's no proof that Torriani was attempting to favour Saronni, of course, but it certainly looked dodgy. In the end, the stage went ahead and alongside LeMond, Visentini laid waste to the opposition. By the end of the day in Foppolo, a ski resort northeast of Milan, Visentini had turned a 70-second deficit into a 66-second lead over Saronni. Once in the pink jersey, the Carrera star wasn't about to be relieved of it. Not even a monstrous performance by Moser in the 36-kilometre time trial to Cremona in stage 18, which he won by almost a minute ahead of Dietrich Thurau, could undo him. A natural climber, Visentini was good against the clock too, and though LeMond made a valiant effort in the race's final mountain stages, there was no beating Visentini. Against some of the world's best riders and a race organiser who had done his best to indulge some old favourites, Visentini won the Giro on his ninth attempt. And against that kind of opposition, no one could say that he didn't deserve it. Twelve months later, however, his entitlement was to be challenged by a very different kind of adversary.

Italy was a country that Roche had learned to love. Growing up in Dublin, he'd seen Milano–Sanremo on television and from an early age admired Italian riders like Francesco Moser. He rode the *Classicissima* early on as a pro, and though it wasn't a race for a climber like him, it was in Sanremo that he first pulled on the Giro's Maglia Rosa. It's a country about which he still talks in tones of obvious fondness.

Speaking now from his home in France, Roche has vivid memories of his first trips to Italy. 'My first impression was that it was different, there was a family atmosphere, the whole system was so relaxed. Back in France [where he'd risen through the ranks as an amateur] there was always a lot of hullabaloo around the races, it's all on the button, really organised, and when we went to Italy, the attitude was more like "ah, it'll be ok". They're more like the Irish,' says Roche, with a laugh. 'The small towns always had loads of people out on the roads, of all shapes and sizes. I'd gone from being an Irish amateur to being a top amateur in France, and then professional. It was a bit of a culture shock.

'Italy felt a bit more amateurish, but the job was always done. In France, it was more professional, there was always hype, stress, pressure, but going to Italy was different, a lot more relaxing. I think it still is. Not just the organisation, everything that was around us. I advised my son, Nicolas, not to go to Italy initially. He had some offers to go there very early in his career, but I always felt that a young kid going there wouldn't go any further. You'd need a really strong character, because the Italians love cycling so much, they love their riders so much, that they'll do everything they possibly can to help them, so that they don't have to carry suitcases or wash their faces after a race. They do everything for the athlete. It doesn't matter what level you're at. If you're a young professional going into that, it's a bad school, because you think that this is what cycling's all about. Whereas in Belgium or France, you're made to carry your own bags, at least until you make a name for yourself.

15. Fausto Coppi's extra-marital relationship with Giulia Occhini scandalised and enthralled the Italian public's imagination. Here, the pair are seen in a rare private moment with their son, Angelo Fausto.

16. No rivalry before or since has captivated the tifosi quite like Gino Bartali and Fausto Coppi. The pair were polar opposites in terms of riding style and personality, and in many ways represented the contrasting faces of a rapidly changing country.

17. Eddie Merckx, known as 'The Cannibal', seen here savaging the opposition on the infamous Passo dello Stelvio. The iconic Belgian won the Giro five times, and might have won a sixth had it not been for a controversial doping expulsion in 1969.

18. There's tough, and then there's Fiorenzo Magni. Italy's 'Third Man', the Tuscan spent much of his career as the runner-up to either Bartali or Coppi. Here he can be seen steering his bike with his teeth, having refused to retire from the 1956 race with a broken clavicle.

19. Francesco Moser's muscular build meant he was never fast enough to dominate in the mountains. Even though the Trentino native only won one Giro, during the 1970s and 80s he was the favourite of Italian cycling fans everywhere.

20. Giuseppe Saronni was a talented sprinter and an accomplished classics rider. He was also one of the dominant Giro stars of his generation. More than anything though, Saronni was Moser's great rival. Their constant feuding delighted race fans and drove them both to incredible levels of success.

21. A gifted rider and the champion of the 1986 Giro, unfortunately Roberto Visentini is these days best remembered for his part in the notorious meltdown that saw the Carrera team at each other's throats in 1987.

22. Ireland's Stephen Roche, the only man other than Eddy Merckx to win the Giro, Tour and World Championships in the same year, pictured after his emotive Giro triumph in 1987, with Roberto Conti, Johan van der Velde and Robert Millar.

23. New kids on the block. The 7-Eleven team took the Giro by surprise in the late 80s, with some performances that changed the European perception of American riders forever.

24. 7-Eleven's Andy Hampsten won the 1988 Giro with a classy overall performance, two stage wins and an unforgettable ride in appalling conditions over the Passo di Gavia.

25. Miguel Indurain pictured with his rivals Claudio Chiappucci and Franco Chioccioli during the 1993 Giro. The big Spaniard wasn't the most electrifying rider, but there's no questioning his record. He is one of only seven riders in the history of the sport to win the elusive Giro-Tour double in the same year.

26. Nowadays famous as an enthusiastic in-race reporter for Italy's national broadcaster, Paolo Savoldelli won the 2002 and 2005 Giri d'Italia, in large part thanks to his fearless descending skills. That trait earned him the nickname Il Falco, 'The Falcon'.

27. *The other greats won more in a year than Marco Pantani managed in his lifetime, but it was always more about quality rather than quantity with Il Pirata. Pantani was loved for his impulsiveness, his daring, and his sense of the theatrical.*

28. As cycling becomes more methodical and dependant on strategy and numerical analysis, Spain's Alberto Contador can sometimes seem like a throwback to the days when a sudden, brave attack was all it took to win a race. He remains one of the most popular riders in the peloton among Italian race fans.

29. By Stage 20 of the 2013 Giro, Vincenzo Nibali had already wrapped up the GC and his first Maglia Rosa. But responding to critics who faulted him for lacking flair, the Sicilian gave an extraordinary individual performance to win on the frozen slopes of the Tre Cime di Lavaredo.

It's a nice thing about Italy, too, that they love their heroes so much, it doesn't matter what races you've won, you'll always find someone who knows you, you'll always be somebody's champion.

'I finished third in the Tour in 1985, and the good thing about the Italian structure is that when you're a leader at a team, they'll all ride for you, they're very good when it comes to teamwork – except for my Giro in '87 of course! But that's a different story. Nowadays, with teams like Sky, that might seem obvious, but it wasn't always like that back then. That was the main reason I wanted to move, independent of any financial side of it. It was a great team with a very good sponsor. Carrera was the first team to have a mobile home, like a camper, for the riders. Everyone else was still using the back of the car, they were the only ones with that kind of mentality for a long time, they were ahead of the rest in terms of structure. There was a different dimension to things with Carrera that I really appreciated. Everyone working for the team was doing it out of passion. In France, it was more of a job, but the Italian masseurs and mechanics loved it and always did an incredible job for us. The most important thing was that infrastructure within the team, that it was capable of rowing in behind me if I was in the lead of a big race.

'Going into Carrera, so many doors were opening up for me after the '85 Tour. Then, with my knee problems, I was held back so that year I ended up riding for Visentini. Maybe that Giro would have been a little bit more for him anyway, because of his track record and the fact that it was in Italy, but within the team, I definitely would have been sharing without my injuries. So I rode for him in the '86 Giro and he won that year. I came into my own at the end of the year, into the winter and the start of the '87 season.'

The previous year had been an *Annus horribilis* for Roche, a

complete contrast to 1985, when he won the Critérium du Dau-
phiné, the Route du Sud, and the Critérium International, and
made the podium at the Tour de France, Paris–Nice and Liège–
Bastogne–Liège. Great things were expected. But after signing
a lucrative contract with Carrera to share leadership roles with
Visentini in 1986, he suffered a serious knee injury when he
crashed during a six-day event at the Paris-Bercy velodrome,
all but ending his campaign before the season had even begun.
Operations allowed him to continue riding, and he lined up
as a domestique for Visentini at that year's Giro, but it was a
disappointing twelve months for the Dubliner. After a winter of
hard work, 1987 got off to a brighter start with a general classification win at the Volta a la Comunitat Valenciana in February.
And having done all the hard work with Claude Criquielion,
he came second at Liège–Bastogne–Liège in a freak finale that
saw the reigning world champion Moreno Argentin sneak up
and pip Roche and the Frenchman after the final corner. There
was another near miss at Paris–Nice, a race dominated in those
days by Roche's steely compatriot Sean Kelly, when a puncture
on the penultimate day cost him the leader's jersey. It looked
set to be a successful summer, and regardless of Visentini's
popularity in Italy, or his close relationship with the team's
management, Roche expected to be given a fair crack of the
whip at the grand tours in light of his obvious form. Unfortunately, not everyone was of the same mind.

The papers all had Visentini as the favourite in the build-up
to that May and, for his part, the defending champion probably
had a right to expect his team to support him as he attempted
to retain the title. The polemics began early on, however. First
blood was Visentini's, in the opening four-kilometre prologue.
But when Roche won the peculiar cronodiscesa, timed descent,
of the famous Poggio climb outside of Sanremo on day two,
trouble loomed. He was 14 seconds behind Erik Breukink in

the general classification, but 15 ahead of his teammate, so Carrera's dominant ride in stage three's team time trial put the Irishman, and not Visentini, into pink. Cycling convention dictates that in the case of a team having two contenders for GC, its full support is given to whoever is wearing the leader's jersey. From Roche's telling, that wasn't the case with Carrera. That could be paranoia, or 20/20 hindsight, seeing signs that weren't really there early on, but it's hard to ignore the possibility that tribalism and personal relationships played a role, because Davide Boifava, the team manager, was from a small town in the province of Brescia, just a short drive to Visentini's home town of Gardone Riviera, on the banks of Lake Garda, which was itself just minutes from the team's base in Salò. The pair had also been teammates, and roommates, in the late 1970s. Visentini was the reigning champ in his own backyard and, parochial as it might have been, it's easy to see how those facts might have swayed reason.

The team's official line was that it had two leaders. The platitudes to the press left out the fact that the pair, both gifted climbers and excellent time trialists, did not see eye to eye. The rider in best form, Roche wanted his opportunity. The man who'd won 12 months prior expected his subservience. They both had a point, and Boifava had a problem. Following the TTT, Roche increased his lead to 32 seconds on the 203-kilometre stage four to Montalcino in Tuscany, but from there it was a dead heat. For the next eight stages, he couldn't shake Visentini.

'Things started to go wrong with Roberto when we arrived at the Giro,' says Roche, looking back. 'We hadn't ridden together a lot that year, he'd been mostly in Italy and I was racing elsewhere in Europe. I'd almost won Paris–Nice until I punctured on the second last day. I won the Tour of Valencia, I was second at the Critérium International – behind Sean, of course – I'd won the Tour de Romandie with three stage wins too, so I was going to Italy with all the boxes ticked. I thought that if Visentini wanted to be the leader, ok, but I had a bag full of results too.

'I was always careful to share my winnings with the team as well. I thought of it as, "If I win £1,000, by the time I pay the tax man I've only got £500 left, whereas if I split it up amongst my teammates, they're getting the full benefit of it." And if I needed them someday, they'd remember that. Visentini never cared about sharing his winnings like that, but I took the social aspect of the team to heart. I thought a lot about how I treated my teammates and about how they were being looked after. Because of that I didn't think that they could just turn a blind eye to me.

'We hit the Giro, and there were signs of tension when I got the pink jersey after the third stage [excluding the prologue, technically stage 1B because the second day's racing was split into two events], a timed descent of the Poggio.

'The guys rode around me the following days, but they were doing it for the team, not for me. With two riders like me and Visentini, normally the tactic would be for one of us to go in any break that developed, but I was in the leader's jersey so I couldn't do it. That was Visentini's job, and he could have been lucky. If it had been a good one he could have stayed away, got the jersey back and win the Giro because of it. But he didn't. He chose to stay on my wheel and just follow me, every day, everywhere I went. Even when groups got away with dangerous riders in them and he should have followed, but he'd wait, and if I moved then he'd follow me. That was the start of it, and I began to think, "What's going on here?"

'On one stage, the time was taken under the red flag at a kilometre to go sign, there was a crash with about 1,000 metres to go, which meant that if I didn't get up quickly I'd lose time.

I was lying on the ground, when Visentini rode right past me and sprinted up the hill to the finish. Luckily enough, I got back on the bike quickly, chased and got back on, but in my opinion he should have been a little bit more concerned, but he wasn't at all.'

The wreck in question was on stage 10, in Termoli, a port on the Adriatic coast. And it was caused by the Dubliner's teammate, the sprinter Guido Bontempi, who, desperate for a win, dove into a non-existent gap and in the process caused a huge pile-up. Roche avoided the worst of it, only to be hit from behind as more riders hurtled towards the finish. The result was some severe cuts, bruises and a haematoma.

Crashes. The weight of the jersey. As he saw it, a clear problem with his team. It all began to take its toll on Roche, and on stage 13's time trial from Rimini to San Marino, his race unravelled. Normally excellent in the TT, over the course of 46 kilometres, the Dubliner haemorrhaged two minutes and 47 seconds to Visentini, the day's winner and the new Maglia Rosa. As he sat at the finish line alone, and the crowd's chants for their Italian hero rang out, Roche struggled to come to terms with what was an embarrassing defeat at the hands of his rival. That, surely, was the end of it.

'It was raining that morning,' says Roche, audibly aggravated at the memory of that most difficult of days. 'But I always did a reconnaissance ride – hail, rain, or shine – I always did the recce on a bike. While I was out, Roberto was in the car, coming up alongside me, asking "Stefano, where's the wind coming from?" From the left. "Stefano, what gear are you using?" I'd tell him. "Stefano, where's the rain coming from?" It's coming down, you know! He kept asking all these questions and it totally wore me out.

'When we got back to the hotel, my ritual was normally to come down three hours before my start to have lunch on my own, with the recce going on in my head, what gears to use, where I'll gain time, where I'll lose it. I'm going over all of this, and it's building inside me, like a pressure cooker, and they'd put Roberto beside me at the table because he was off at a similar time. So the two of us are sitting there, and he's still asking questions. I felt like saying, "Roberto, if you wanted to know all this, you should have done it yourself." But I said nothing, and he kept wearing me down, pumping me for this information.

'I went to the start, and on the line I knew it wasn't going to be my day. My legs were totally empty, I was wasted. I knew it would be a very long day. At the finish, I knew Visentini had won, that he'd taken over the pink jersey, and there was no one there from the team to give me a towel or say "Hard luck, tomorrow's another day." There was nobody consoling me, I was just left there, like I'd never done a thing in my life. That was very upsetting.

'Back in the hotel, I was watching the last of the Giro coverage on TV, when they have a little chat after the stage, and Roberto was there, talking to the journalists. They asked him, "Now that you've won the time trial, you've got the pink jersey on your back, you've shown you're stronger than Roche, so is the deal now that he'll ride for you now and when you go to the Tour, you'll ride for him?" He said straight away: "No, no, Roche is riding for me here, but I'm not going to the Tour, I'm going on holidays." So I thought, that's a bit cheeky but at least he's being honest! He expected me to ride for him, but not to count on a payback, so I wasn't too impressed. There and then, in the room with Eddy Schepers, we started looking at the race ahead because we were still nine stages from the finish.'

Visentini's vacation has since become the stuff of legend. An earlier promise to support Roche in the Tour wasn't worth the paper it was printed on, and as far as he was concerned, he'd be celebrating Giro number two on the beach come July. To his detractors, this was typical of a man said to be preening and patrician. Whether that's fair or not depends on your point of view. The son of a wealthy undertaker, Visentini was the antithesis of a typical cyclist. He'd had it easy, liked to race motorbikes and ski, and only turned to road racing when it became apparent just how good he was at it. As a junior, he was Italian and world champion, duelling it out on a regular basis with Saronni, and reputedly fighting off a host of attractive young women while he was doing it. Talented and handsome as he most certainly was, communication wasn't his forte, and in his aloofness, his uncomplicated self-confidence could easily be interpreted as arrogance. In a contemporary interview with the Corriere della Sera, the country's most widely read daily, Roche described his teammate thus: 'He's a rider with class, but very few words. I've tried to talk to him, but he responds monosyllabically. And he's never happy, he's always complaining.' The man himself once memorably told a journalist: 'I didn't think I had any rivals, but then I realised, my biggest adversary was myself.' So he had an ego, wasn't much of a talker, and came from money, but these are hardly crimes. That July holiday was a serious offence, though, at least to Roche, and one he took very seriously. The Irishman was known to be one of the most tactically adept and calculating riders in his heyday, and he wasted no time plotting his next move with Schepers, now the only rider on his team that he could trust.

'We were trying to figure out if the Giro was really over, or if there was still a chance. And one thing we knew was that we couldn't attack Visentini, because he was my teammate. We couldn't attack, but we could be on the lookout for a good break, and if I could get into that, Roberto doesn't chase, and I'm really strong and can stay away ... maybe there was a chance.'

That chance came quickly, on stage 15, a day full of climbing that would finish with an ascent to Sappada, a small German-speaking town north of Venice and just a stone's throw from the Austrian border. For Visentini, a day that had started like a dream, with him back in pink and in control, was quickly turning into a cold, wet nightmare. The stage started quietly on the sun-drenched coastline of Lido di Jesolo, but as if in sympathy the weather changed with Visentini's fortunes and by the time he reached the route's first climb, up the Forcella del Monte Rest, some 90 kilometres from the finish, it was clear that he had a problem. When a small group got away, Roche saw his opportunity. He'd bridge across to cover the break-away, a common move to make when a team is protecting its GC leader. In this case, however, the thin veil of altruism was fooling no one. Carrera's cold war was about to get very hot.

'A group got away,' says the 56-year-old, with the kind of élan that used to characterise his racing. 'We had nobody in there, which wasn't a problem in itself, because there was nobody dangerous involved, but generally when you're leading a race and a group gets up the road, you want to keep the advantage down, so at some stage you put your team on the front to chase, unless you've got a rider up there with them. It was a long climb, with a long descent afterwards, so I went towards the front and thought that I'd try to close the gap as I'm descending. It meant that, if I closed the gap, great, there'd be no breakaway. But if the guys behind me didn't follow me, I could get across and you'd never know what could happen. So I just had to wait and see.

'I went over the top with Eddy, getting faster and faster, but I never looked over my shoulder, for obvious reasons. There are some days, on a descent like that, you have to take risks. Other days it's just like poetry in motion. That day, I went down the descent like I'd done it a 1,000 times before, every corner was just so neat and clean. Guys like Visentini, they were great descenders, but that day I left them all behind me. Once we caught the group on the front, it was 25 kilometres to go on the flat, then there was a climb, I was worried that it might be a bit suicidal. If the guys behind me caught me on the final climb, with teams like Panasonic, and there's a fight to the finish, I'd be spat out. But I just thought, "I'm here now, let's see what happens."

'At the same time, the team car pulled up beside me, and asked me, "Stephen, what are you doing?" I told them I was defending the jersey, that there were three guys breaking away on the front with nobody from my team. They just told me, "That wasn't your job." I said, ok, but we need someone here, and they said, "Yes, but it's not your job. You better back off." But why back off, I asked, with the guys I was with, it would have been an easy ride. They said, "Steve, you don't understand. That descent, you went down so fast that there were guys on the floor, hanging out of trees, everywhere. It's totally disorganised." I said, great, I can win the Giro. Again, "No, you don't understand. Wait for Roberto." I said that Roberto should sit in, wait for a bit until Panasonic and the other guys get organised and they'll chase me down. Of course, I was hoping they wouldn't, but that was the tactic. But again, "No, you don't understand. You have to stop." That was it. I said, "Tell Roberto to stop riding behind me, or if he does, he better leave something in the tank, because when he catches me I'm going to go again. It's his choice."'

The eight-kilometre climb on Monte Rest was narrow and winding, a cramped back road, nestled in thick tree cover. It was Visentini's turn to raise the stakes, and he chased with all his might, but Roche hadn't yet played all his cards. Little did Carrera know, but the riders in the breakaway with him were on his side. Jean-Claude Bagot, who was riding for Roche's future team, Fagor, had won on stage six, but that victory might have been Schepers'. Sensing civil war in his own team, however, the Belgian had traded the win with the Frenchman in return for a favour down the road.

'That shows you the kind of mentality he had,' says Roche of his friend. 'He never rode for himself, it was always for the team and his leader. He was very generous that way. I brought Eddy with me to the team in '86. He rode a similar sized bike to me, a very clever guy, he was a domestique to some top riders, and wasn't fuelled by his own success, he was fuelled by the success of the team. A great guy.

'He did a good job for Visentini at the Giro in '86, but at the end of the year Carrera didn't want to keep him and Roberto didn't open his mouth. I told them that I was getting my form back and that I'd need someone like Eddy. He appreciated me defending him, so he knew if he helped me I wouldn't just leave him. We had that confidence in one another.'

The summit of Monte Rest was Roche's Rubicon. Everyone now knew that he had no intention of riding for Visentini and that he still had designs of his own on the Maglia Rosa, and so, as the road pitched downward, he risked it all on a fearless descent. Roche caught Ennio Salvador, from the Gis team, and the pair worked together before teaming up with Bagot further on. They built up a lead of almost a minute and a half, but after another descent, they arrived in a valley and faced a long stretch of wide, straight road. But as Carrera chased, Visentini remained like a deer in the headlights. The Irishman's brashness had caught his Italian rival by surprise. He was no longer able to hold Roche's wheel, and Roche was no longer shadowboxing. The attack had knocked Visentini off-kilter, and as the rain poured down, he lost his nerve, and his strength.

In most grand tour battles between two evenly matched talents, defeat is like death by a thousand cuts, a gradual wearing down of an opponent over days or weeks. But that day to Sappada was a single, vicious and fatal stab at Visentini's Giro. He was said to be a highly strung and sensitive character, and the trauma of that stage proved too much to handle. Carrera chased, but Visentini collapsed, worn out by his one-time teammate's tenacity and perhaps by the psychological strain of it all. Up front, the two insurrectionists pressed on with a small group, knowing full well that Boifava was sending the rest of their team to wipe them out.

Even when Bagot flatted and Roche's lead dwindled, Visentini had no response. The breakaway was absorbed by the chasing pack, but when another group countered, the 1986 Maglia Rosa imploded. Roche joined the aggressors, among them his friend Robert Millar. An alliance of Italian riders again closed the gap, all hungry for their own glory, but as the day approached its final kilometres on the Cima Sappada, Visentini was getting weaker, first struggling up a relatively gentle gradient in an easy gear and then almost coming to a stop when the incline spiked on a 16 per cent wall, a couple of kilometres from the top. His two-minute, 42-second lead over Roche wasn't going to be enough. Nowhere near it.

'I remember looking back and seeing the whole Carrera team, 30 or 40 seconds behind, riding on the front trying to catch me. I was possessed. When we hit the final climb, they caught up, and another group went away. I was riding beside Roberto, he was struggling. Eddy was with me too – encouraging me, telling me to hang on, not to blow – when Roberto started going backwards. A few minutes later, the car comes up again, and tells Eddy to wait for Roberto. Eddy told them, "No, Stephen's leading here, Roberto's going backwards and I can't do anything for him." After that, he turned around to me and said, "I just covered for you here, but you better cover for me tonight or else I'll be out of the job!"

'He stuck with me and paced me on the climb, until about a kilometre or so before the top, which was still three or four kilometres to the finish, there was another small group going away, with Tony Rominger, Steve Bauer and a few others. Eddy told me that he couldn't do any more for me and that I had to go, because this was where I'd win the Giro. I buried myself for those last few kilometres.'

After a short descent to the line, a young Swiss rider by the name of Tony Rominger raised his arms, erroneously thinking himself the day's victor. In fact, the Dutchman Johan van der Velde had quietly slipped away before the main groups merged on the final climb and rolled in alone, victorious, 46 seconds ahead of anyone else. The day's real *victor ludorum*, however, crossed the line a physical and mental wreck, not far behind Rominger. The scale of triumph wasn't immediately clear to the 27-year-old, but when race officials rushed over and hurriedly bustled him towards the podium, the penny dropped. He was back in pink.

'I was back in the lead, five seconds ahead of Rominger. Visentini lost six minutes. So the good side of it was that the team couldn't send me home because I had the pink jersey on my back, but the bad side of it was that at the finish, Roberto told everyone that I had attacked him, and because I couldn't talk to the press, he gave his side to everyone.'

Davide Cassani, now more famous as a TV commentator and for being the current manager of the Italian national squad, was a young domestique for Carrera at the time, and he remembers Sappada, and the split in the team, vividly.

'It looked like Roche had attacked to take the jersey, so the order arrived to push to bring them back. Visentini was really nervous. We started to pick up the pace, but once Roche realised that his own team was working to pull him in, he started to push even harder too. You can imagine what the journalists thought.

'The only one who didn't pull was Schepers, who was Roche's roommate. Now you can understand what a nice team we had,' he says, laughing. 'We managed to catch Roche on the final climb, but then Visentini had a crisis and Roche was able to take the jersey. I was sharing with Visentini and when we were back at the hotel he was furious ... but I just looked forward. For us domestiques it was important to win the Giro – a little for the honour, but also for the pocket – and there we were, we went from having first and second to risking losing it all.'

Roche couldn't talk to the press because he'd been ordered to his room by a furious Boifava. Having started the day with the top two GC places and a three-minute lead over Rominger, the team's Giro now lay in tatters, with a lead of just five seconds over the Swiss, one deeply unpopular rebel in pink and the pre-ordained champion a physical and psychological wreck. No one entertained the idea that it had been Boifava, rather than Roche, who had ruined Carrera's day. If the team had played the game in the usual manner, rather than chasing their own rider and dragging the entire peloton with them in the process, the Irishman might have stayed away all day and built an insurmountable margin.

'Visentini collapses in controversy,' declared the headline in La Stampa, one of Italy's oldest daily newspapers, their correspondent Gian Paolo Ormezzano neatly observing that 'Roche had come good and turned bad.' That day shook Roche to the core, but unlike Visentini, he used it to fuel a remarkable comeback. A planned contract extension was torn up. His teammates even shunned him in the hotel restaurant, leaving him to eat in his room. Shocked by what he saw as his team's duplicity, and by the reaction of race fans, the least popular man in Italy grit his teeth, suffered the slings, and set out to prove everyone wrong. There were meetings with journalists in secret, and an impromptu appearance on Italian television when he barged onto the set of the post-race analysis, leaving the legendary commentator Adriano De Zan somewhat lost for words, but the hostility wouldn't let up.

'The team was very disappointing. I'd been generous all year, I'd left a lot of money on the table, I always treated everyone well, in a stage race I'd never put them on the front and tell them to ride for the sake of it, I'd always wait until the right moment tactically, I never made them ride for nothing. It hurt me a lot. First of all, the time trial hurt, because no one was interested in me, to help me or console me, that was hard to swallow, to feel like I was on my own. I'd been generous all year, and at the Giro I was in pink for 10 days, I felt like I'd done everything right. Roberto hadn't done a thing for me all year, so I couldn't understand what was going on. Something wasn't right. I felt like I'd missed a chapter in a book.

'If it hadn't happened,' he says, pensively, 'if you described that same scenario to me and asked me what I'd do, I'd say "Go home". But at the time, I just thought, "Do or say what you want but I'm not going anywhere."

'But things were bad; my masseur was making me food because he was afraid of someone trying to poison me, and my mechanic wouldn't let my bike out of his sight because he was afraid someone would try to sabotage it. It was very tense. Rolling down to the start, I'll never forget all the people, the banners saying "Roche go home!" or "Roche Bastardo", all kinds of horrible slogans. During the next stage people were punching me going up the climb, so I had to have a chat with Robert Millar so that I could have him and Eddy blocking me left and right, because I had no one else. They kept the crowds back, but some fans were putting rice and red wine in their mouths and spitting it at me as I got close. It was terrible.'

That might seem melodramatic, but in the murky world of professional cycling, anything was possible. In 1983, a scandal erupted when two hotel waiters claimed that they'd been offered two million lire to slip a powerful laxative into the food of Saronni and his Del Tongo team. After tipping off the police, the waiters organised a meeting with the conspirator, Giovanni Arrigoni, the owner of the FIR wheel company, who was arrested in front of a delighted pack of photographers. Arrigoni sponsored a team, and wanted his rider in pink. And the team involved? Inoxpran, Carrera's previous incarnation. There was no suggestion that Visentini knew about it, but he must have winced when he saw the front page of the *Gazzetta* on 6 June 1983, screaming, 'Scandal: They tried to poison Saronni!'

Undeterred, Roche pressed on. With the help of Schepers, he held on to his lead in the Dolomites, working with his friend Millar to fend off Erik Breukink's advances. The team came around towards the end, but the tifosi didn't. The abuse continued, and when a crash at the end of stage 20 caused chaos, angry fans jumped the barriers and attacked an exhausted Roche before the police could get to him. Millar was rewarded with a win on the final mountain stage to Pila the next day, securing the Scot second spot on the podium and the climber's jersey as a bonus. And in the final time trial to St Vincent, a spa town north of Turin, Roche did what had been beyond him in San Marino and rode to a comfortable victory. Visentini retired with an injury before the start. Perhaps speaking figuratively about his time in Italy, he called that stage win, 'the nail in the coffin'.

With just weeks to go before the start of the Tour, Roche left his team to celebrate without him and drove through the night back to France, possibly stealing the occasional glance over his shoulder or in the rear-view mirror to make sure that they weren't chasing him, even then. He was on the precipice of greatness, and Visentini's career lay in ruins. He never won another race, and upon retiring in 1990, he turned his back on cycling for ever.

12

1988: FEAR AND LOATHING IN LOMBARDY

The 1988 Giro was a beast. Vincenzo Torriani no longer had to cater to Francesco Moser, and so the veteran director had a field day with the mountains. The 3,579-kilometre route was shorter than in 1987, but included some 30 categorised climbs on 15 climbing stages, balanced out with four time trials in the hope that the drama could be stretched right to the final day's individual race against the clock in Vittorio Veneto. One thing it did not include was a rest day, though the peloton was eventually granted some respite when the 11th stage from Parma to Colle Don Bosco was cancelled.

The race was also notable for the cosmopolitan list of challengers. There had been no Italians on the podium the previous year and the prognosis wasn't great for the 71st edition, either. Though he was now rid of his old rival Moser, Giuseppe Saronni was in decline. And there was no telling if Roberto Visentini, the champion in 1986, had got over the trauma of losing to Stephen Roche the previous June. A new generation of Italian riders were on the horizon, but it was still too soon for the combative Claudio Chiappucci, who would dominate the mountains of the Giro and the Tour in the early 1990s, or the gifted Gianni Bugno, who would retire a decade later with a Maglia Rosa, back-to-back world titles and with wins at both Milano–Sanremo and the Ronde van Vlaanderen to his name. To the chagrin of the tifosi, it looked like being another race for the foreigners.

Spain's Pedro Delgado and France's Jean-François Bernard had rounded out the podium in Paris the year before with Roche, who wisely decided not to defend his Giro title. In form, the Swiss rider Urs Zimmermann was always a threat, as was the young Dutchman, Erik Breukink. And then there was Andy Hampsten, back with 7-Eleven and back at the Giro after a two-year hiatus.

No longer the unknown quantity that had lined up at the 1985 Giro for his first race as a professional, the 26-year-old had made a name for himself by finishing fourth at the 1986 Tour and winning the Tour de Suisse twice on the trot. Big things were expected.

Hampsten picks up the narrative. 'By '88, I'd established myself. But we started the season with two leaders, myself and Raúl Alcalá, who was riding really well. We were better that way, we raced for whoever was in form. We were all out of our minds happy to be back at the Giro, we're a pretty big team now, not kids any more. We were experienced cowboys! We loved racing in Italy. We all wanted to race there. So I went into the Giro hunting. If I had the form, I was there to win it and the team was behind me. But we were there to have fun and to ride a race we all loved and respected, and if I was going to lose time, I wasn't going to lose two minutes trying to hang on to my overall position, I was going to lose 10 and then try to win stages.

'I hadn't had a great spring, but I was getting better and I was fourth in the Tour de Romandie a couple of weeks before.

I was coming around, and the Giro was going to be a long race, with huge mountains towards the end. Now that Moser wasn't there any more, he didn't need to be catered to and they were making up for it – including this huge stage over the Gavia.'

More on that anon. The racing got off to a bright start, with Bernard taking the Maglia Rosa in the opening time trial, followed three seconds later by Tony Rominger. The Frenchman held the GC lead until stage four, when the unheralded Massimo Podenzana somehow crept away from the uninterested peloton to ride into the Adriatic seaside town of Rodi Garganica more than five minutes ahead of everyone else. Podenzana would hold on to the pink jersey until a major shake-up on stage 12, when his fellow Italian Franco Chioccioli took over.

Chioccioli was part of Saronni's Del Tongo team, but after the opening days of the race it quickly became clear that he was a better bet than his captain. The 28-year-old Tuscan had impressed on stage six, beating Hampsten and Zimmermann on a hilltop finish in the Apennines at the ski resort of Campitello Matese, around 100 kilometres north of Naples. That attack put Chioccioli into second place overall and, as the peloton's heavy hitters started to jostle for position, very much in the frame for overall victory.

The 12th stage had four categorised climbs and finished at Selvino, in the mountains outside Bergamo in the province of Lombardy. Del Tongo controlled the racing, but on the final ascent Hampsten launched an attack to stamp his authority on the race and got away with Delgado, who was out of contention for the GC but still eager for stage wins. The American star pipped the Spaniard by 11 seconds, with his other main rivals a few more seconds behind, and though it was Chioccioli who took the leader's jersey, it was clear that Hampsten, riding into incredible form, was going to be tough to beat.

Fast forward to Sunday, 5 June. Stage 14 from Chiesa

Valmalenco to Bormio. At just 120 kilometres, it was short on distance but long on drama, even before the peloton saw the weather forecast. That day has since become legendary, one of the Giro's most indisputably brilliant – and unquestionably ludicrous – days in the mountains. The route first crossed the Aprica before heading up the Tonale pass towards the fabled Passo di Gavia, which had featured in the Giro just once before, back in 1960 when the great Charly Gaul was the first to tame it. Even in clement conditions, it's the kind of climb that inspires fear, but on the morning of the stage, the riders awoke to the promise of a frozen nightmare. It was the kind of theatrical, reckless stage that fans point to when asked why they love the sport, and in an age when rider safety and common sense rightly prevail over irresponsible excitement, exactly the kind of careless racing that we're unlikely to see again.

'Looking at the profile, the Gavia stage seemed alarmingly difficult because it wasn't too long, and those stages are often the most dangerous,' says Hampsten, recalling a day that would define his career.

'I was friends – still am – with Gianni Motta, who loves Americans, and he came right up to us at the start and told me, "Andy, you're going to win the Giro and you're going to do it on the Gavia." And he said he'd told all the other teams the same thing. He told me that the other guys weren't respecting how hard that stage was going to be, that with modern cycling it wouldn't be a problem. But we listened to him.

'Our team doctor, Massimo Testa, had grown up in Lombardy, so he knew the pass and he'd driven over it, and he said the same thing – that it's just crazy, that everything Gianni said was true. The road is nuts, it's not switchbacks, it's tricky, really steep, it wasn't paved. Nobody in their right mind has to go over it; there are other roads. But we were looking forward to it.

'I'd won the uphill finish two days before riding away from everyone. At the time I thought they were playing a practical joke by not chasing me down! I'm sure my legs hurt, but I felt like I could do whatever I wanted, we were racing so well, it was looking great.

'The morning of the 14th stage, the race was to go down through the valley, over the Tonale pass, with a little descent, a false flat to Ponte di Legno and then up and over the Gavia, with a 25-kilometre descent to the finish. The start wasn't very high up, but it was snowing, and I was distraught. This was supposed to be my day. But they checked the roads and the organisation said that the stage would go ahead, so we were still on. The weather was unfortunate, but it was also an opportunity.

'I put more pressure on myself than anyone else did – the team just said, "do what you can." But everyone was prepared, the whole team went shopping and we bought every bit of warm clothing we could find. Every rider made a musette full of clothes for the top of the climb. The plan was just to get to the bottom in one piece because we knew it would be worse going down than going up. The stakes were high. The team did a great job not putting pressure on me, and all of us let the soigneurs put lanolin, the sheep's wool fat that's impervious to water, all over our bodies. Not just our legs, everywhere! We knew we'd be soaked to the bone, so we wanted to waterproof all of our skin and to just think about the descent – I wasn't racing to the top of the Gavia, I was racing to the bottom. I had to go hard to the top, but keeping in mind that seconds on the climb could be minutes on the descent. It was all about averting disaster. I was the strongest, I'd won two days before, riding everyone off my wheel, that would have been the tactic in good weather, but now it was all about the descent.

'At the start of the climb, I wasn't sure what to do. My rivals knew I'd attack, so it wasn't a surprise, but I went and it worked. So with 14 kilometres to go, on a 14 per cent grade, it was narrow but it was a good road, even before it was paved. There were no potholes, it was compacted dirt, not dangerous at all, and with the snow, it was a really good surface. I attacked hard and I got away from my rivals. I could see them on the switchbacks, but they couldn't ride together and as it went on, I got over my own fears of the day because I knew that it was hard on everyone.

'I saw how everyone else looked, and Franco Chioccioli, who had the Maglia Rosa, looked like a ghost. They were shell-shocked before we even started climbing. On the descent from the Tonale I had to let go of my bars because I was shaking so hard from the cold. Part of my tactic of attacking with 14 kilometres to go until the top was that I'd just stay a little bit warmer. It wasn't 100 per cent up the climb, I needed to save energy to be clear-headed for the way down, but I went hard. I went at my pace, stuck to my plan, but then at the top I took a plastic rain jacket that I couldn't get on! I couldn't get my neoprene diving gloves through. I should have stopped and put it on in 15 seconds, but I was a pro, I had to stay on my bike and keep riding, swerving around in the snow, and lose a lot of time.

'Erik Breukink caught me at the top. He didn't put on a jacket. He's Dutch, and on Peter Post's Panasonic team, he's supposed to be tough. On the way up I'd put on a wool hat and a neck gaiter pulled up over my nose, and with my Oakley Factory Pilots, I had no skin visible. With the plastic jacket over the wool jersey, I was warmer. I was wet, and the jacket flapped about, but it was a lot more comfortable. I thought I'd follow him, but he wasn't descending well so I took over and never looked back. And in the blowing snow, I didn't know where anyone was. I was descending, pedalling in the same gear, I think a 53 x 14, there's icicles steaming off my bike, I'm feathering my brakes. I've been back there many times since and I know it couldn't have been very fast, but I was just focused on keeping my legs moving and not freezing up. I cannot describe how cold I was. I grew up in North Dakota, it's really cold there, far from the ocean, six months of winter, we all knew about the dangers of frostbite and hypothermia. I've had frostnip, losing some skin from my nose or my ears, but the Gavia was different. It wasn't that I was going to get frostbite, but my core was really low, I was losing my reason as we got colder and colder. All I thought about was balancing my bike.

'As we passed through Santa Caterina, we picked back up with the race organisation and the cars. There'd been no lead motorcycle or race director ahead of us on the climb, no one visible. They'd all been waiting for us in the town to see if the race made it. The communications were relayed through a helicopter, I think, but it couldn't fly that day. So we go through the town and the race cars are all there and it looks like a bike race again. At that stage, Breukink wasn't that far behind me and he's more aerodynamic without the flapping jacket, so he passed me with seven kilometres to go. It looks like I'm asleep, but I remember seeing him and trying to get on his wheel, but I couldn't. I just used him as a rabbit, and held him there. I could have got rid of the rain jacket and tried to catch him, but I probably would have crashed trying to take it off and to be honest, I might have fallen over from being too cold. I wasn't out of mind, but it was close. I knew I was far colder than I should be. I was racing for warmth, for the hotel. I don't know what I'd have done if I saw the team hotel before the finish line!

'I crossed the line in second. My team car came in after me over the line and parked 50 metres from the finish. There were no barricades or anything, the spectators were freezing, but they were mountain people and they love the Giro – and the fact that the race didn't quit, they weren't going to. They were so excited.

'They bustled me into the team car, I had a bag of dry clothes ready in anticipation, they gave me some tea, the car was running with the heater blazing. They saw I needed a moment on my own, I was shaking, crying, hysterical. They came to check on me and I was in a rage – not in anger, just emotion – because I'd realised how dangerous and challenging the day had been. I wasn't making any sense, but they understood, it's part of racing, I was going through a lot! But after a few minutes, I was mad because they didn't even tell me how it went, where I was in GC, did I take the lead, what was going on ... and they told me, "Andy, no one else has even crossed the line."

'Then I heard the loudspeaker, "Here's Roberto Tomassini, third place, four minutes and 39 seconds." I think I had a minute on him at the top of the climb, so our plan had really paid off. Then it's Franco Chioccioli, who had the leader's jersey, coming in seventh, but more than five minutes down, so huge differences. By then, I was really coming around! I wasn't shaking so much any more, I was just thinking, "Get me out of this car, man! Get me a jacket, where's the podium?"

'One of the great joys of cycling is being on the podium on a day like that, holding the flowers and seeing your teammates cross the line. It was a beautiful moment, in the bucketing rain, watching these guys who were freezing, but they got to see me up there with the Maglia Rosa. I'd won already, I wasn't the new kid like in '85, I was wearing the pink jersey, it was fantastic.'

That day on the Gavia has since become infamous. Aside from the 7-Eleven riders, almost everyone in the peloton was completely unprepared for the appalling conditions. Most crested the summit in short sleeves, with no thought given to protecting themselves from the elements. There were reports of brakes frozen stiff, and derailleurs clogged up with ice, so it doesn't take too much imagination to picture the physical horrors suffered by the miserable peloton. Johan van der Velde, who had been first over the top just ahead of Breukink, Hampsten and Chioccioli, ended up stopping and waiting for more clothes. He then chose to tackle some of the descent on foot, and eventually lost 47 minutes to the leaders. Chioccioli was left distraught by the experience. He still maintains that the stage should never have gone ahead, but Hampsten disagrees. Everyone had underestimated just how horrendous the weather would be, but there was no excuse for some of the biggest teams in the sport being so poorly prepared.

'I don't think anyone groaned about the fact that Breukink won or that I got second, but there was a lot of talk about being treated like dogs and about the fact that the stage should have been cancelled, that we shouldn't have to race in the cold. I think it's part of the sport. I don't want to be falsely modest – I liked what I did, I thought it was cool. But no other team was prepared for that. They had no warm clothes, no one had adequate support for their riders at the top. And now, in every race, every rider has a rain bag with their name on it in the back of the follow car. That started on the Gavia with 7-Eleven.

'We had always experimented. In 1984, when I was still earning more money from other jobs than I was as a bike racer, I worked for a company in Colorado that made outdoor clothing, and they hired me because I went into their store asking for stretchable materials, I wanted to make my own rain jacket. It wasn't just the sponsors, we always looked for things to help us. Our team just wanted to keep us going, and if the sponsor didn't make what we needed, we used another one. They always protected us. They bought us ski gloves. Most of us raced or trained in Colorado – we knew what was coming. They didn't want us to get sick, and the guys who weren't racing for time stopped to change. No other team had that. Johan van der Velde, I didn't see him the whole day, he stopped and his team handed him a plastic cap and a plastic cape and just said "Go". He already had hypothermia. Our team, as I heard it, gave him some hot tea, pretty much as first aid. There's no reason not to do everything you can to take care of yourself, but 7-Eleven was the only team at that point that was intelligent and flexible enough to adapt to the conditions.

'The weather wasn't a complete surprise. It wasn't a major technological advance, it was just common sense. We were always thinking about anything that could help, whether that was sunglasses or warm gear, whatever innovations we could. Why suffer more than you have to? It's fine to tell your grand-kids about how hard it was, but if you're 30 minutes down because of it, it's an intellectual lapse not to prepare for that.'

Thanks to his heroics in that blizzard, Hampsten held the Maglia Rosa, but there was still more hardship in store.

'The next day, the Stelvio was cancelled. There was no way over. We drove over part of it, so it was a very abbreviated stage. I suffered every pedal stroke and lost track of the leaders, but I opened up some more time on Breukink. The day after, the weather was so bad that we stopped in a tunnel in protest. We came up with a good idea with the organisers, because they promised us that on the other side it was all sunshine, 18 degrees Celsius, and the forecast for the finish in Innsbruck was really good. So with some common sense, we still had three or four hours of riding left, we decided to put on extra clothes, ride to the top, descend as a group, stop again, change clothes again and then race to the finish.'

If only it had been that simple. Cue drama.

'As soon as we agreed, Chioccioli attacked! Everyone's swearing. My team chases him down with Breukink and his Panasonic team, and when we catch him, he's browbeaten into playing along. Then at the top, my team warned me, "Come straight to the front, make sure that you're on the edge of the descent so you can see everything." And sure enough, Chioccioli attacks again. So Breukink and five or six Panasonic guys are right after him, and I had to take the first few corners at full tilt, risking everything because it was dangerous in the rain, but I needed to be on that train because I knew, I'd raced with those guys, they were big, powerful riders and total badass bike racers. We caught him, but at that stage, the game is on. We had an agreement, but he'd broken it, so it was chaos and we were back racing and we were going all out all the way to the finish.

'As we're descending, we'd been warned about this temporary wooden bridge, and as we cross it, I hear someone crashing behind me. First I thought, "God, this is terrible, we shouldn't be racing like this, we should have neutralised the whole thing," but then I turn around and see that it's Franco Chioccioli! He was the only one who crashed.'

More than a match for his rivals and the weather, the only thing that stood in Hampsten's way that final week was the looming threat of the final time trial. A climber in the purest sense, the American knew he'd need a comfortable lead before the final 43-kilometre TT to Vittorio Veneto. Breukink was undoubtedly better against the clock, and so too was Zimmermann, who'd been working himself back into contention. Luckily for the GC leader, stage 18 was a short, uphill time trial, a *cronoscalata* to the locals, finishing in Vetriolo. He romped to victory, 32 seconds ahead of Visentini in second place, more than 50 seconds ahead of Zimmermann in fourth, and more than a minute ahead of Breukink behind him. With the 20-second win bonus, it put him one minute and 51 seconds ahead of his Dutch rival. Barring disaster, the Maglia Rosa, and with it a place in the history books, was Hampsten's.

Zimmermann, down but not out, tried one more roll of the dice the following day, launching an audacious attack with the Italian Stefano Giuliani. The pair built a big enough gap to put the Swiss in pink, and after toiling incessantly for two weeks, 7-Eleven were in no condition to respond, especially not when doing so would leave them exposed to a counter from Breukink. As is so often the case, to win this Giro, Hampsten and his teammates had to be prepared to lose it, first.

The gamble paid off. The Panasonic and Del Tongo squads had their own interests to think about, and so set about chasing down the breakaway before it was too late. Giuliani took the stage and Zimmermann climbed up to second in the GC, but Hampsten was still almost two minutes ahead, with only two more flat stages and the time trial to go. In the end, he didn't even have to worry about that, because brimming with confidence and in the form of his life, the American put in an uncharacteristically strong showing against the stopwatch on the race's final day, finishing two minutes behind the powerful Lech Piasecki but, crucially, only 23 seconds back from a clearly enervated Breukink. Two months after his 26th birthday, and just three years after making his professional debut, Andy Hampsten was the first non-European winner of the Giro d'Italia. And as an added bonus, he took home the Maglia Verde as the race's best climber, too.

13

MARCO PANTANI

To see Marco Pantani at his best was to believe in magic. He was a vicious climber and a fearless descender. His attacks were things of terrible beauty, mesmerising for their virtuosity and for their violence. Marco was a fighter, with a flare for the theatrical. And more than anything, Marco was unpredictable – as prone to implosion as he was to explosive acts of virtuosity. Marco was mercurial. Has there ever been a rider who deserved that adjective more than Pantani? We use it to mean unpredictable and ever changing, deriving that sense from the planet, which has the fastest orbit around our sun. But the root of the word comes from the Roman god, a messenger from the heavens, the patron of speed and of expression – and also the soul's guide as it travelled to the underworld. You'd struggle to invent an epithet more fitting for the winner of the 1998 Giro.

With the possible exceptions of Coppi and Bartali, no rider has left a more indelible mark on Italian cycling than Pantani. And even though he's been dead for more than a decade, a newcomer to the sport would be forgiven for thinking that he was still the biggest star in the peloton, such is the prevalence of flags, banners and graffiti dedicated to him along the roadside during every Italian race.

But Marco wasn't meant to be a cyclist. As a child, he'd dreamt of playing football for AC Milan, and only turned to the bike after becoming frustrated at being left on the bench by his local team's coach. He was too small, said the trainer. No good for sports. That diminutive stature might have been a hindrance on the pitch, but on the road it was an advantage and it quickly became clear to the local cycling club that they had a real talent on their hands.

His home town, Cesenatico, is typical of much of the Adriatic coast: vibrant, sometimes garish, built for the sun and coloured happy for holiday-makers; it's charming, even as its glory fades and the paint peels. The old town is built around a canal and a dock full of fishing boats. By dark, you can see the not-so-distant glow of Rimini to the south, with the gleam of its nightlife seeping out over the water. People go to Cesenatico to sunbathe, and to party, and it was an odd place to find one of cycling's greatest climbers: born by the seaside, but made for the mountains.

There's a museum dedicated to him on the edge of town, beside the train station. The Fondazione Marco Pantani. It's quirky, with a life-size, two-dimensional model of Marco, in perpetual motion thanks to a small motor, climbing to nowhere. The museum celebrates the best of Italy's last truly universal cycling superstar, with walls covered floor to ceiling by jerseys and by photos of Marco. He liked to paint, and some of his pictures have been hung reverently alongside football memorabilia and old newspaper cuttings. His custom motorcycle takes pride of place, in what is both a touching tribute to a lost talent, and a temple to turn-of-the-century kitsch. Just down the road from the Fondazione, however, there's a stark reminder of the darker side to Pantani's life: namely, his tomb. Cesenatico's cemetery is swarmed by as many as 50,000 cycling fans a year, who come to pay tribute to their late hero, who would now be in his late forties.

Marco grew up on the shore, but his future lay elsewhere, and so did his family's roots. They'd originally come from Sarsina, a small town that was 50 kilometres inland from Cesenatico, in the foothills of the Apennine Mountains. It was the home of the Roman writer Plautus, who was said to have been a great influence on William Shakespeare. It is also a popular pilgrimage site for Catholics possessed of personal devils and wishing to pray to Saint Vicinius, who was famous for performing exorcisms. Demons and drama in the mountains – there could be no place more fitting.

Eddy Merckx won more in a year than Pantani managed in his whole career, but that doesn't matter. He was about quality more than quantity, and his victories were made all the more special by his obvious frailty. And though time and again all the evidence suggested that he'd never truly fulfil his immense potential, his talent was such that you couldn't give up on it. Pantani was something to hope for. In him, the Italians saw their next Campionissimo, heir apparent to Coppi, although sadly in the end they had little more in common than the fact that they both died too young. People loved him for his weaknesses as a man and his strength as a rider, for the way in which he overcame both internal and external struggles. His victories were exalted, mythologised, precisely because he wasn't like Merckx.

Pantani is the last rider to win the coveted Giro-Tour double and one of only seven to ever do so. The others were Coppi, Jacques Anquetil, Merckx, Bernard Hinault, Stephen Roche and Miguel Indurain. But his 1998 Giro win, and the Maillot Jaune that followed in July, were grand tour wins that had for so long seemed beyond him. Great things had been expected of

Pantani from a young age, but two serious crashes threatened to derail his career before it had even got going.

By the 1994 Giro, the little climber from Cesenatico was already well known to the sport's more informed followers, having won the Girobio – the amateur equivalent of the Giro – in 1992, but he was still an unknown quantity in the professional peloton. Ostensibly part of the Carrera team as a gregario to Claudio Chiappucci, Pantani was ready to have the spotlight all for himself, and vowed to retire from cycling if he failed to make an impression that May in the mountains. The 24-year-old did not disappoint. His Corsa Rosa started well, and he climbed his way into the top 10 early on, before losing five minutes and 47 seconds to Evgeni Berzin in a time trial on stage eight. He was out of contention for the GC by the time the race reached the Alps – but not out of ideas. At stage 14's start in Lienz, Austria, Pantani was in flying form. The 235 kilometres to Merano were billed as the most spectacular of the race, a showcase parcours intended to flaunt some of northern Italy's most stunning scenery while also pushing the likes of Miguel Indurain to their limits. Undaunted by the route or by the opposition, Pantani attacked in what would become his trademark, impetuous fashion, launching himself out of the main chasing group and into the torrential rain, a kilometre from the summit of the Passo di Monte Giovo. As he crested the climb, Pantani hung his body out behind the saddle, getting his centre of gravity as low as possible and tucking into an incredibly aerodynamic – and dangerous – position for the chase, something he'd learned to do to limit his weight disadvantage on the descent. It took 13 kilometres to catch and pass the day's leader, Pascal Richard, and from there it was still another 30 to the finish. Gianni Bugno and his Team Polti-Vaporetto drove the hunt, but Pantani stayed away, hammering, toes down as always, on the pedals, hugging the corners, embracing the risks. He took his maiden victory as a professional on one of the Giro's hardest stages, ahead of Claudio Chiappucci, Miguel Indurain, Bugno and the race leader Evgeni Berzin.

'Marco was never afraid of being on his own,' says his first trainer, Giuseppe 'Pino' Roncucci. 'He had the courage and the ability to attack in a race and stay out for 50km. All of his life's journeys were like that. On the front, alone.'

The next day, almost seven million Italians tuned in to see young Marco lay waste to the peloton and draw blood from the hitherto invincible Indurain. Stage 15 was a brute, and featured a hellish combination of the iconic Stelvio and the Passo di Mortirolo, a climb that many argue is the most challenging in Europe. The Italian Franco Vona from GB-MG-Technogym, a teammate of the previous day's victim, went on an early break and was the first to summit the Stelvio and by the midway point of the stage, he'd built up a lead of six minutes and 40 seconds over Berzin. Pantani kept his powder dry as the peloton began its ascent of the Mortirolo from Mazzo di Valtellina, but began to test his adversaries as the gradient worsened. Indurain chose not to respond, but the Russian race leader, emboldened by the Maglia Rosa, followed his attacks for a kilometre before succumbing to exhaustion. Marco climbed alone for the next 10 kilometres before passing Vona and reaching the apex of the pass alone, having ravaged the pursuing pack. It took him just 43 minutes and 53 seconds to complete the 12.4 kilometre climb, beating the record set by the 1991 Giro winner Franco Chioccioli by two minutes and 17 seconds. On the descent, Pantani allowed himself to be caught by the Colombian Nelson Rodríguez and Indurain, keeping them company until the final slopes of the day, where he set a blistering pace up the Valico di Santa Cristina before plunging down to the finish in Aprica almost three minutes ahead of his teammate, and ostensible leader, Chiappucci. Incapable of a response, Indurain had looked almost frozen in time as Pantani soared away. It was time for the world at large to sit up and take notice. Almost two thirds of all Italian televisions were tuned in at that moment – as well as millions more across the continent. With his courageous, back-to-back victories, Marco had entered the sport's elite and endeared himself to the Italian public.

Had it not been for the experience and steady nerves of his teammate, Moreno Argentin, Berzin's bid for Giro glory could have come undone later in the race, as Marco's naïve belligerence continued. But the Russian held on, finishing the final stage from Turin to Milan with a GC lead of two minutes and 51 seconds over his young Italian rival. Pantani, for his part, must have felt that he'd won himself, because he had not only outperformed Chiappucci, but also beaten Indurain, the winner of the previous two Giri, to second place on the podium by 32 seconds.

Tragically, that was probably the last time we saw the full expression of Marco's potential. The physical problems, crashes and internal struggles that would gravely affect his later years were just around the corner. The following year, he was the favourite for the Giro, but while training in the hills around San Marino, not far from his home, a Fiat Punto knocked him from his bike, causing lacerations but no fractures or breaks. The driver was from Cesenatico, and was appalled to find the local hero bloodied on the tarmac. Convalescence robbed Pantani of his early season form, but he still expected to start that spring's Giro in Perugia on 13 May. Two days before the Grande Partenza, however, a training ride left him in excruciating pain, and he was forced to abandon. He returned for the Tour de Suisse, but at the Tour de France, a change of crank length exacerbated an old pelvic problem – an asymmetrical gait and the erroneous diagnoses that attempted to correct it had almost ended his professional career before it began – causing him so much suffering that he nearly abandoned. Marco was almost back to his best, and his bronze at the World Championships that autumn convinced him that it was worth trying his luck at Italy's final one-day events of the season, and he planned to ride the Milano–Torino on 18 October to fine-tune his form before the year's last Monument, the Giro di Lombardia. He should have stayed home. Confusion between race officials and local police meant that a car was able to slip onto the race route on the Corso Chieri, in the suburb of Reaglie, just outside Turin. On the twisting, narrow road, there was no way for the driver or the riders to see one another in time, and when they met, Marco was flung skyward, along with Davide Dall'Olio and Francesco Secchiari. His Carrera bike was in pieces, but worse damage had been done to Pantani. There were breaks to his shin and in the ankle and knee of his left leg. Fragments of bone protruded from his calf. A difficult operation left him with an external splint holding his leg together, with five bolts screwed through his skin. It also left one leg seven millimetres shorter than the other, and cast huge doubts over the future of his career. The splint would stay in place until February 1996, and the scars, both physical and mental, remained for the rest of his life. It wasn't enough that he had to fight his rivals and the mountains, now Marco was fighting his maimed body, too.

He was a different man when he returned to racing a year later. As a younger rider, his nickname had been L'Elefantino, the Little Elephant, because of his big ears. Understandably, he wasn't a big fan. In 1997, however, his diamond earring, goatee, gaunt features and the bandana he wore to cover his bald head lent him another kind of appearance. That of a pirate. Il Pirata was a different rider: still capable of brilliance, but wounded, and wracked with self-doubt.

Another crash caused him to abandon the 80th edition

of the Giro, but his immense talent finally delivered the following year. After taking the Maglia Rosa on the seventeenth stage, Marco looked in control, but his performance lacked the panache to which his fans had become accustomed. They didn't have to wait long. Stage 19 was classic Pantani, a rabid assault on the race that left no doubts about what they were witnessing: this was history in the making. Alex Zulle, the two-time Vuelta a España champion who would later become mired in the Festina doping scandal at the 1998 Tour, had led the GC early on but was a spent force by the time the race reached its final week. Pantani's other main rival, the Russian champion of the 1996 Giro, Pavel Tonkov, had won the day before on a short stage from Selva to the Passo di Pampeago in Trentino. He was better on the flat than Pantani, and could look forward to making time on the Italian in the penultimate day's time trial. Once the Mapei rider limited his loses to Il Pirata in the high mountains, the Giro would be his.

If Marco wanted to keep his Maglia Rosa, he had to risk it all on that year's final climb to Montecampione. But try as he might, he couldn't shake the Russian all day. With less than three kilometres to go, it was the final roll of the dice for Pantani, who launched one of the most memorable and mesmerising attacks in recent cycling history. Marco tossed his bandana to the road, his signal that this was do or die. Next went the glasses, and his water bottles. He always told reporters that he did this in order to shed as much weight as possible, but there was a touch of theatre to it, too. And before his final eruption of defiant, expressive energy, he threw his diamond nose stud into the bushes. Later he'd say that he could feel the weight of it pulling him down, and that he'd had a vision of his late grandfather, urging him to get rid of everything he didn't need. There was no way back from all this. His genius was always characterised by irrevocable gambit. Trying desperately to hold on, to survive Pantani's onslaught, Tonkov looked like a beaten prize-fighter, battered and blind, grasping for the ropes. If this had been boxing, the referee would have stopped it, but in the high Alps of Lombardy, the Russian found no respite. The gradient increased, and with it, Marco's ferocity. He needed a statement win, and to take at least half a minute from Tonkov, who could still count on his superior ability in the TT to claw something back. By the summit, he had 57 seconds, and as he crossed the line, time seemed to slow down. He held his arms out, as if on a crucifix, with his exhausted expression and his closed eyes turned to the sky, in what is now one of the Giro's most iconic images. This was Marco's masterpiece, expressionistic and in vibrant colour. In the end, he even beat Tonkov in the TT. Superb form and imperious confidence would carry him to glory later that summer in the Tour, and it was as if Marco was riding the crest of a wave of endless possibility. And no one could have known how soon that wave would break. Or how hard.

Though it seems wretchedly unfair, Pantani is probably most famous for what came after his outstanding Giro-Tour couplet. A career that should have delivered so much more joy disintegrated into sorrow and squalor and, eventually, death.

The 1999 Giro was all but decided when Marco's life was thrown into turmoil. By the time the race reached Madonna di Campiglio, Pantani already had one eye on the Tour. His lead over Paolo Savoldelli was five minutes and 38 seconds – and had been growing by the day. By the morning of Saturday 5 June, however, that lead, and Marco's life, had been undone. Tests after his victory on the previous stage had revealed a 52 per cent haematocrit level in a blood sample, 2 per cent more than the safe limit that he himself had helped the UCI to set. He was removed from competition for safety reasons. It wasn't a ban. It wasn't even an indictment. But to Marco, it was a death blow. The two-week suspension would rob him of his second Giro title, but he was free to start the Tour's prologue in Le Puy du Fou on 3 July. Marco chose not to.

What happened afterwards is the stuff of soap opera. Immediately after the news broke, Marco went to ground as a media storm threatened to consume him. Debates about clean sport aside, the final GC of the 81st Giro is laughable when you look at the riders allowed to continue. If he was dirty, he couldn't have been any more grimy than those around him. The entire top 10 have since been caught up in doping scandals of one form or another; in fact, the start list was a who's who of EPO users, for it was the debut Giro for a young Danilo Di Luca, Italy's doper par excellence. His samples have since gone missing. Other tests from the same race seemed to contradict the UCI's findings at Madonna di Campiglio. Years later, a mafia enforcer turned informant claimed that the Camorra crime syndicate in Naples had rigged the whole thing as part of a betting scandal – something that sounds outlandish until you see how deeply they were able to affect other sports. A football betting scandal in 2012 was estimated to have made the crime syndicate more than €2 billion, according to Italian police, and in 2016, the *Gazzetta* revealed fresh allegations about widespread match-fixing in Serie B and the country's lower leagues. After that Giro, depression got the best of Pantani. There were truncated attempts at a return, but his heart was no longer in it. He felt that he'd been singled out, and as he succumbed to drug addiction, anger and self-pity snuffed out whatever fight was left in Cesenatico's little pirate. Marco died a little less than five years later of an apparent overdose, after a cocaine-fuelled binge had left him all but unrecognisable and alone, in a grubby hotel room up the coast from his family and friends, in a dark corner of glittering Rimini. He was 34, and it was St Valentine's Day.

Writing his obituary, the always eloquent Gianni Mura said: 'Marco Pantani began to die that morning of '99, on Madonna di Campiglio. He did not accept the positive, he did not accept anything of what happened to him. Many other riders, caught up in doping affairs, stopped and restarted. Not him. He, the King of the climbs, also specialised in the descents. Down into Hell, into the artificial paradises, into hiding from public opinion, journalists, judges. He became more and more isolated, his solo attacks became rarer. And every so often, in this or that newspaper, on this or that TV show, they'd cry out: Marco come back. They were right to appeal, because cycling without Pantani was, and is, a soup with absolutely no flavour. It's a stage without a leading man, full of actors willing but unable to give a jolt to the heart of the public. Pantani was able to do that very well, it was his great specialty. Pantani on the climbs was the equivalent of an acrobat without a net. A ritual, with almost mystical rhythms. He was like a samurai. Leaving the others destroyed.'

COLLE DELLE FINESTRE, PIEMONTE

'The hill of windows.' A fitting name for one of Italy's most visually stunning mountain passes, a road that offers postcard-like views at almost every turn, climbing from Meana di Susa, three quarters of an hour from the metropolitan buzz of downtown Turin, through a thick tangle of forest and tightly bound bends towards an untouched, elevated paradise, worlds away from the city below. First commissioned by Louis XIV in the eighteenth century, the Colle delle Finestre connects the Susa and Chisone valleys to the largest Alpine fortress in Europe, Forte di Fenestrelle. And though it's one of the newest additions to the Giro d'Italia's portfolio of theatrical climbs, it is already one of its most famous.

The former Giro director Carmine Castellano first stumbled upon the road in 1995 and immediately knew that it could be his legacy to the race, but it would take a decade before the Corsa Rosa finally scaled the Finestre's 45 hairpins. The main problem facing Castellano had been the route's horrible surface. It was, in his own words, 'an impassable goat track'. But with the 2006 Turin Winter Olympics looming, the

Piemonte regional government had money to spend promoting itself – and there were few better ways to do so than by unveiling a modern cycling classic as the 2005 Giro's final mountain stage. The road was improved, but without losing the distinctive, sooty gravel that added to the challenge of an 18.5-kilometre climb that reaches an altitude of 2,178 metres with an average gradient of over nine per cent.

This was a climb to hark back to the Giro's golden age, unpaved and irrationally difficult, a special find that echoed the great innovations of Vincenzo Torriani decades before, on the Stelvio and the Gavia. Better still, after 18 stages the fight for general classification was still precariously balanced between the leader, the 2002 Giro winner Paolo Savoldelli, one of the all-time great descenders, who was also sitting on a two-minute lead, and Gilberto Simoni, champion in 2001 and 2003 and by some margin the superior climber. A minute further back in the standings, Venezuela's José Rujano and a young Danilo Di Luca were close enough to feature, too.

The route took the peloton over Sestriere first, and by the foothills of the Finestre, Savoldelli was struggling to keep up with Simoni, Di Luca and Rujano. The attacking trio were lighter and better suited to the mountains, and the Maglia Rosa often suffered from allergies. There was no way he could match the inhuman pace that Di Luca was setting. Simoni was the virtual race leader, but his rival tried to remain unfazed. It was up to the mountains to decide their fate.

Luck was on Savoldelli's side. The young Colombian Mauricio Ardila, whose Giro had come undone several stages earlier, started to pull. Whether he did so out of pride or because his race director was an old friend of Savoldelli mattered little to the Maglia Rosa. He was gaining on the aggressors, just when Di Luca was pushing the limits of his implausible performance.

Simoni was still leading the provisional GC at the summit

of the Finestre, but the impetus was with the man in pink, now descending, back doing what he did best, with the tiny Ardila glued firmly to his wheel. As the road rose for the final climb back up Sestriere, the gap fell. Di Luca was spat out the back leaving Simoni exposed, with only the work-shy Rujano for company. With 10 kilometres to go, the gap was one minute 37 seconds – with a 20-second bonus guaranteed to the winner. With eight kilometres to go, the gap was one minute 20, half a minute less than Simoni needed even if he took the stage. Then, with four to go, the cunning Rujano played his hand, attacking his breakaway partner with a dash to the finish to take a victory that was both cruel and brilliant. Simoni was 22 seconds behind, followed by a distant and destroyed Di Luca. It took Savoldelli one minute 53 seconds to cross the line, but he'd done enough. He still led by 28 seconds. The 2005 Giro d'Italia was his.

14

A DECADE OF DIFFICULTY

After Hinault, Fignon, Hampsten and Roche relegated them
to the sidelines in the late 1980s, Italy's riders returned to
primacy in the 1990s, winning five of the decade's 10 races.
While Miguel Indurain came twice with the Banesto juggernaut
to steamroller the opposition, and Evgeni Berzin, Pavel Tonkov
and Tony Rominger scored wins for Russia and Switzerland
respectively, Gianni Bugno, Franco Chioccioli, Ivan Gotti, and
of course, Pantani, gave the home fans plenty to be cheerful
about.

But as the new millennium came and went, as Stefano Gar-
zelli and Gilberto Simoni came to prominence, the tragedy
of the country's most loved sportsman played out in front of
millions, on the front pages of newspapers and on television
screens everywhere. And he wasn't the only problem. Everywhere you looked, there was scandal. To borrow a phrase that
the writer Roberto Gervaso coined while discussing the swamp
of Italian politics, cycling remained on its feet only because it
didn't know in which direction to fall.

Pantani's ruination cast a long, melancholic shadow across

Italian cycling. For some, it was the tipping point. And so they simply switched off. As a pastime, road cycling remained a staple of everyday life, especially in rural areas and the north, but the professional side of the sport was just more trouble than it was worth.

At the end of July 2007, the *Gazzetta* journalist Candido Cannavò wrote an exasperated column, declaring that he'd asked around in the cycling world for the name of a single rider who, hand on heart, people could swear was clean. All he'd got in response had been deafening silence. But a week later, a letter arrived on his desk, one that the paper duly published. It was from a 23-year-old named Miculà Dematteis, who rode for the Tenax-Menikini team at Pro Continental level, what was at the time the sport's second tier.

Dematteis' epistle was a moving portrait of the life of a young athlete, the struggles of his every day and the satisfaction he gained from doing something he loved, something that was hard but, he thought, worth it. The only time he saw a doctor, he said, was when he had a cold, and then it was the local GP. His final paragraph read:

'Cycling is a magnificent sport, made of strength, power and tactics. I'll continue to train hard, believing and giving everything I have to climb onto the podium and honour my sponsor. It won't be easy, but when it happens it will be payback for all the sacrifices, and it will prove that my idea of clean cycling exists. You've probably never heard of me, though I'm sure if you ask around and mention my name, you'll find people who believe in me. I cannot guarantee the others.'

That podium never came, and by the time that Dematteis had celebrated his 24th birthday in November of that year, it was clear that no offers of employment for the following season would be coming either. His career was over before it had begun. Being clean had got him nowhere.

One rider who did have a contract with Dematteis' team for the following season was Danilo Di Luca, who we now know was an all-star when it came to doping. Di Luca was from a small town in Abruzzo called Spoltore, in the hills above Pescara, and while he had an impressive career, winning three Monuments and the 2007 Giro d'Italia general classification, the stories of performance-enhancing drug abuse followed him around like a bad smell. Time and again, his ties to the Abruzzese entrepreneur Valentino Sciotti meant that the rider's doping transgressions were overlooked by teams desperate for sponsorship money from the cycling-mad businessman. He was suspended the same year that he won his Maglia Rosa, and again in 2009, when he tested positive for a Continuous Erythropoietin Receptor Activator (CERA, an advanced form of EPO) on two separate occasions. Defying all logic, Di Luca was still able to slither his way back into the peloton every time, and in 2013 he was back in the limelight when Sciotti forced him upon the managers of the Vini Fantini team that he sponsored, sparking some very public denunciations of Di Luca by his new bosses. Regardless of the protestations, the patron got his way and his friend, the rider they called the Killer, began the 96th Giro with a team he'd never met before. Before the race's end, he was popped again, finally receiving a lifetime ban, when an out-of-competition test taken in April came up with traces of EPO. He'd given the sample two days after his previous racing ban was lifted. Lance Armstrong, for once in his life talking sense, tweeted: 'Knowing I have no cred on the doping issue – I still can't help but think, "really Di Luca? Are you that fucking stupid?"'

Di Luca, of course, was just a symptom of the real problem. He was under pressure for results, from himself and from his sponsor, and having grown up in a sporting culture where pharmaceuticals were a part of everyday life, he returned time and again to a form of preparation that to him seemed normal, something that everyone did, and something that was an unexpressed but universally understood requirement of being a good professional bike racer. He comes from a generation of riders that either denies they ever saw any drug use, or defiantly asserts that it would be impossible to win a modern grand tour without the assistance of illicit stimulants. Generally speaking, what camp they're in depends on whether or not they have ever been caught red-handed.

Of the 16 riders to finish on top of the Giro podium in the years between Franco Chioccioli's win in 1991 and Vincenzo Nibali's first Giro victory in 2013, Damiano Cunego is the only one not to have served, at some point in his career, a doping ban or a suspension related to haematocrit levels, or to be connected to Francesco Conconi, Michele Ferrari or Eufemiano Fuentes, three of the doctors at the heart of cycling's EPO and blood-doping pandemic. That isn't to say that they're all guilty, obviously, and Dr Conconi in particular is still a respected sports scientist, but it is regrettable that the sport was allowed to become so corrupted that two decades worth of records can be called into question, if not with direct evidence, then at least as a result of suspicious association.

The really poisonous part of the problem, however, was not that there were a few glory-hungry cheats at the top of the sport. It was that for many struggling riders, doping became the only way to keep their jobs. It's easy for an armchair observer to pontificate on the life choices of a multi-millionaire athlete who was clearly talented before he took drugs, but it's worth sparing a thought for the second-tier domestiques who could start their careers on as little as €25,000 a year – a pittance for the sacrifice and suffering that goes into being a pro cyclist. They mostly come from poor backgrounds, with little education, and the prospect of making it onto a World Tour team, or at least a Continental one, is life-changing not just for them, but their families as well. It would be interesting to see how many of the people who erupt into a blaze of indignation on social media every time a cheat is exposed would risk an injection if it meant the difference between abject failure and a moderately successful, if unremarkable, career.

None of this was new. Henri Pélissier was boasting to journalists about the drugs he took in the 1920s. Fausto Coppi used to say that he only took pills when necessary, and when the interviewer would enquire as to when that was, he'd reply wryly: 'Almost always.' Gastone Nencini, the eccentric Lion of Mugello, who liked to paint and to chain-smoke whenever he wasn't riding, blood doped in the 1950s. Jacques Anquetil was an unapologetic user of stimulants, and when race organisers tried to force him to submit to urine tests, he hired a lawyer and launched a legal attack on what he said was 'a threat to individual liberty'. Eddy Merckx tested positive for amphetamines on several occasions in the 1960s and 1970s. In the 1980s, on at least one occasion Bernard Hinault refused to partake in testing and Laurent Fignon was a vociferous opponent of tighter controls. We could go on all day, but the point is that collective negligence, not the actions of individuals, unpalatable though they may be, is what almost killed the sport. In 2001, the UCI released a bombastic document entitled 'UCI – 40 years of fighting against doping (1960 – 2001)' that was so fanciful, propagandistic and self-congratulatory that it would have made a Soviet-era editor at *Pravda* wince. This was at the same time that the organisation's president, Hein Verbruggen, was doing everything in his power to cover Lance Armstrong's tracks. The sport's governing body, teams, race organisers and fans – everyone seemed to be OK with doping, until suddenly they weren't.

As case after case unfolded, Italy's long-suffering sporting public lost their appetite. Much like the plight of hooligan-ism and match-fixing that was crippling the country's football league, cycling's grubby image was keeping all but the most dedicated fans away. People wanted to believe in the good, but every time they did, it was thrown back in their face. Through-out the 2000s it seemed as if cycling, and in consequence the Giro, could do nothing to clean up its act. It remained a spec-tacle and there were some memorable moments, but few of the victories seemed credible. It looked like the rot was ineradica-ble. The great melodramas of Alfredo Binda and Fausto Coppi were replaced by a grotty soap opera in which second-rate actors like Riccardo Riccò risked their lives by giving them-selves DIY blood transfusions. And at a time when there were more screens in people's lives than ever before, people turned off. Viewing figures for the 100th anniversary in 2009 were the lowest they had been for a quarter of a century.

COLLE DELL'AGNELLO, PIEMONTE

Stage 19 of the 2016 Giro d'Italia, and Vincenzo Nibali was out of form and out of ideas, a shadow of the gutsy, unpredictable racer adored by the Italian tifosi, and nothing like the dynamic champion who had won the 2010 Vuelta a España, the 2013 Giro, or the 2014 Tour de France. Only five other riders have won all three grand tours, and the press were slow to write him off, but deep into the Corsa Rosa's second week, criticism was building. The Dutchman Steven Kruijswijk had surprised everyone with his resilience, growing more comfortable in the Maglia Rosa every day. And if he cracked, went the common consensus, it would be the affable Colombian Esteban Chaves who would profit. Nibali was out of the running. Nibali, some argued, might even be finished.

What had happened, no one knew. Paolo Bettini, the 2006 and 2007 world champion, was one of several to publicly question his compatriot's decision to change his pedal crank length so late in his career. Emilio Magni, the team doctor at Astana, blamed a surprise physical problem and promised extensive testing. Nibali's coach, Paolo Slongo, insisted that he'd take his rider home if he was sick, saying that they didn't want to 'scrape the bottom of the barrel', while Giuseppe Martinelli, Astana's veteran team manager, said it was 'a difficult moment, the most complicated of [Nibali's] brilliant career'.

The 31-year-old Sicilian, normally a picture of composure, looked ill at ease, and more than a little upset at the flak fired his way by the Italian papers and a lot of cycling fans. 'Leave me in peace! I've nothing to say. You can see how I'm going,' was his response to the media after stage 16. 'Why do you want to keep hurting my pride? I'm already in bits.'

He'd silenced the sceptics before, ending a disappointing 2015 season with a remarkably defiant win at Il Lombardia to make him one of very few modern stage racers to also win a one-day Monument, but this time it seemed different. It would take a miracle to turn this around. Or so we thought. In fact, all it took was a stroke of luck, a rival's mistake under pressure, and then his own tenacity, that visceral resistance to failure that sets the great apart from merely the good.

The Colle dell'Agnello is among the most irresistible climbs in Europe, and at 2,744 metres, also one of its highest. It stretches more than 50 kilometres from its base in Piasco, ascending 2,178 metres to its pinnacle and the French frontier, sweeping through bucolic vales and dense pine forest, the very picture of the Italian pastoral idyll, on long false flats, before revealing its true, brutal character, with the lone peak of the Monviso piercing the sky overhead. The highest point of the Alps along the Franco-Italian border, it's an unconfirmed but popular belief among the locals that it inspired Paramount Pictures' famous logo. Which is fitting, because the drama that unfolded in its shadow in May 2016 would make any Hollywood scriptwriter proud.

With snow covering everything but the tarmac, the race meandered upward towards 2016's Cima Coppi, past hoards of fans braced against the cold and enveloped in a thick fog that dulled the senses, limiting sight and sound to just a few blurry metres. Michele Scarponi, 2011 Giro winner turned *gregario di lusso*, lost his breakaway companions early on the climb and rode alone to the summit, almost six minutes ahead of the peloton and of his team leader, Nibali, but not in search of personal glory. He was waiting for a surprise.

Close to the summit, Chaves attacked, covered by Kruijswijk and then by Nibali, and the trio stuck closely to one another as the road crested. Then, in an instant, the entire race changed. Kruijswijk, from northern Europe's Low Countries, struggled to hold the wheels of Nibali and Chaves, both excellent descenders. And after misjudging the apex of a long, sweeping turn careered off the racing line and violently into the snow banks on the road's edge, flying head first over the handlebars in a dramatic somersault. Luckily, the 28-year-old avoided injury and was soon on his feet, but as both he and the neutral service mechanic struggled to get his bike back on the move, his lead in the general classification vanished, as Chaves and Nibali, at ferocious speed, plunged down towards the Queyras valley and into France. There were still more than 50 kilometres to the line in Risoul, where another difficult climb awaited, but the Agnello had blown the 99th Giro wide open.

It was the moment that Scarponi had been waiting for, and the 36-year-old came to a virtual stop on the day's finishing slope where he sacrificed his own ambition in the service of the most unlikely victory in recent Giro history. Nibali, reinvigorated, launched one attack after another in the closing kilometres, against the persistent ripostes of Chaves. The Italian eventually broke free, finishing 51 seconds ahead of everyone else. The pink jersey belonged to the Colombian, but Nibali's was a greater prize: absolution after almost three weeks in hell. The next day, another stage packed with mountains, he would erase Chaves' 44-second lead and take the Maglia Rosa for himself with just one flat stage to go. That too, was a tactical masterpiece, and Scarponi again played a huge part, but at that point the momentum had shifted. The Agnello changed the entire race, like only a truly great climb can, and it would be difficult to come up with a stage in recent memory that better illustrates just how captivating the Giro can be.

15

THEN AND NOW

These days, the *Gazzetta dello Sport* is part of the RCS Media-Group, an international publishing conglomerate based in Milan that owns titles around the world, most notably the *Corriere della Sera*, Italy's most widely read newspaper, and *El Mundo* and *Marca*, two of the dailies in Spain. The company's headquarters is tucked away on a quiet street in the northeastern suburbs of Lombardy's capital, a leafy area known as Crescenzago, one of many small towns that have been absorbed into the city's perpetual sprawl over the last century. The road is named after the group's founder, Angelo Rizzoli, who made his fortune with his eponymous publishing company, and RCS's large, low-rise block of buildings stands in the centre, between the thoroughfare and the Lambro river. Inside the complex, the courtyard is ornamented with several large pillars displaying a selection of the *Gazzetta*'s most iconic covers, from the lurid green of the paper's first edition to Italy's Fabio Cannavaro holding the World Cup aloft in 2006, and the jubilant yellow celebration of 'Roi Nibali' after his 2014 Tour de France victory. All colourful towers of heady summer memories against the sodden grey of an autumn afternoon in Milan.

In a first-floor office overlooking the square, Mauro Vegni is busy putting the final touches to the presentation of the 100th edition of the Giro d'Italia, surrounded by mementos from a lifetime in cycling, including a replica of the race's iconic *Trofeo senza fine*. Born in 1959 outside Siena, Vegni grew up in Rome. After university, he began a career in cycling that would eventually lead him to his current position as the director of Italy's most important race, only the sixth in its 108-year history. Originally, he'd been a footballer, with little interest in bike racing, but by twist of fate, his affections shifted thanks to the suggestion of a very influential neighbour in the Italian capital.

'Franco Mealli lived nearby,' says Vegni. 'He was a Roman who organised several races, including the Tirreno–Adriatico, the Giro del Lazio, he was one of the biggest in Italy after the *Gazzetta*. He convinced me to forget about football and took me with him to see some races, and with that, I started following cycling out of curiosity.

'While I was at university, I gave him a hand whenever I could. That was the end of the 1970s, beginning of the 1980s, and later he made me a proposal to work in the cycling world. So in February '83 I formally joined his company, working full-time on the cycling calendar. I gained experience working at various national championships on the track and on the road, at the Tirreno–Adriatico and a lot of other stage races too, like the Giro di Puglia, the Giro della Provincia di Reggio Calabria, the Giro dell'Umbria. We did the amateur Giro d'Italia as well.'

Unfortunately, the legacy of organisers like Mealli has been somewhat neglected by the sport's followers today, but once upon a time he and others like him were cornerstones of the sport in the provinces. Cycling was in his blood – his uncle Adelino raced against Gino Bartali and both his brothers, Marcello and

Bruno, were professional riders – but Franco chose a different route, towards organisation and roles in large events like the 1955 World Championships, held in Frascati, in the hills south of Rome, and the capital's 1960 Olympics. By the 1970s Mealli had built up an impressive portfolio of beautiful races across central and southern Italy, many of which are, sadly, no longer with us. So significant was he, in fact, that people often referred to him as the 'Torriani of the south', in reference to the long-serving Giro director of the time. He remained passionate about cycling until his death in 1997, when *La Repubblica* lamented the passing of '*l'ultimo alfiere di un ciclismo antico*', the last standard-bearer of old cycling. His influence on Vegni was a lasting one, but eventually both he and his protégé realised that the sport had undergone seismic change and that Mauro's future lay elsewhere.

'In 1994, I was the director of the UCI World Championships in Agrigento, Sicily. RCS came to that Worlds to see if it would be possible for me to join their organisation.

'By that stage at the start of the 1990s, Mealli was having health problems and I didn't really want to continue on my own. There was too much to do, too much at risk, all the hours focused on publicity, the payments, you don't know how much … So, in the end, after talking to Mealli, I took the decision that if the *Gazzetta* was interested, it was better if I went there. They also wanted to acquire all of our races, but to do that they needed someone else in organisation and support, because it basically doubled the amount of race days that they had, so Carmine Castellano had asked them to take me. From '95, I was there. Castellano was in charge and I stood in for him when needed, but I wasn't there to "*tagliare l'erba sotto i piedi a nessuno*".' (In Italian, to cut the grass beneath someone's feet means to force someone to move or to cause them problems.) 'The idea was that he was a mentor, and that over time I might replace him when he retired.'

Both the pace and the scale of change seen by Vegni, or indeed anyone working in cycling over the last few decades, has been striking. For better and for worse, the way in which the sport is organised hardly resembles even the era of Francesco Moser and Giuseppe Saronni, and has nothing to connect it to the era of Fausto Coppi, other than a journalist's occasional cliché and the nostalgic concoctions of marketing managers. But while Mealli might have been the last standard-bearer of the country's cycling golden era, his understudy seems attached to elements of the past, even as he plans for the future, and whenever the subject of the sport's transformation comes up, he seems intent that while the developments made have largely been good things, we should not throw the baby out with the bathwater.

'Like everything in life,' he says, 'over time there are always changes. Cycling, once upon a time, lived on passion and voluntary help, but today, if you want to do it properly you need to act like a business. The sport has changed substantially in that regard. There's a great desire from sponsors for an event like the Giro d'Italia, in terms of the images, television etc. And technically, on an instrumental level, everything has changed, there has been a revolution in terms of the bikes, the clothing, everything. In terms of security, too. In the old days, if you watch the footage, the riders arrived at the finish surrounded by crowds, with maybe two or three policemen to manage the fans. Now, there have to be barriers, fencing, controls ... there's an incredible amount of attention paid. And rightly so, because for the riders accidents can happen at any time.

'There's been an extreme change too in terms of human relationships. Years ago, with a telephone call you could make deals and create events. Now there are contracts, lawyers and legal departments, accountants. But the whole world has changed, and cycling, as such, had to change too.

'If I think of cycling back in the 1970s, it seems almost pre-historic compared to today. It's natural, but if you asked me what I missed about back then, I'd say the human aspect. The values. I miss that a bit. For the rest of it, change is normal and I've been a part of it. But yes, I miss the older values in every context, from the racing, but also in relationships behind the scenes. Back then, when you talked to a manager in a team, if he said yes, it was yes. Today, it's never yes. One moment they'll tell you that they're coming with a champion, the next minute he's sick. That used to never happen. In the concept of a person's word, there was a lot more respect.

'When we talk about change in Italian cycling, we can talk about revolutions and we can talk about digressions. To give you an example, without wanting to criticise anyone, up to the 1990s, we were at the peak of cycling. We had more teams than anyone, we organised more than anyone and we had more champions than anyone. And we still had track cycling, maybe not at the same level, but still among the best. In the last few years we've seen a bit of a renaissance, but there was a hole of 10 dark years in between. Today, we have Vincenzo Nibali and Fabio Aru, which compensates a lot, but we don't have top classics riders. There seems to be some revival, on the track as well, but we're a long way from where we were.

'I don't think it would be difficult to return to that level. It's not as if the other countries are better or worse than us. Now there are more countries involved, especially from the English-speaking world. Back in the day, it would have been one of the highlights of the year to see an Australian rider for example and you'd never expect them to win a race. Now, the anglophone world has been able to develop champions, and cycling has been globalised. And with that, there are now a lot of riders with different experiences.

'We Italians, for example, are more like purists for the road bike and for road racing, but these days lots of guys come from mountain bikes or something else and they've proven themselves to have the quality. The whole world has opened up. If you look at the knowledge in cycling now, like rider diet – it used to be sandwiches in the morning that had been made by the masseurs the night before.'

Perhaps the only concern with all of this change is its effect on the sport's financial sustainability. Cycling has a long, inglorious history of operating in an unstructured, often hand-to-mouth manner, but in an era of ever-increasing professionalism, the uncertainty that plagues so many of the sport's events and its teams can no longer be ignored. A few decades ago, teams got by on a relative shoestring. The main costs were rider contracts, with small staff and a few vehicles to support them at races. Now, most of the World Tour's big teams could fill a hotel parking lot with their fleets of buses, mechanics' trucks and team cars. Most have a dedicated chef, who increasingly want to have mobile kitchens to ensure that they can provide the best possible nourishment to the riders during gruelling stage races, where backwater accommodation often comes with limited cooking facilities and questionable levels of hygiene. Team Sky, famously, even has a van full of washing machines and driers. To a layperson, these might seem like small, inconsequential details in the context of professional sport, but for all of the glitz and glamour that comes across on TV at something like a grand tour, it remains very much a sport of modest resources.

Back in 1982, the Giro's future hung in the balance. A financial crisis at Rizzoli pulled the rug out from under Vincenzo Torriani, who was trying to run the event with just four full-time employees. The 65-year-old had been at the helm since the 1940s and was, according to his peers, a genius of invention and of race organisation, but thanks to the sport's shaky economic footing, he found himself in charge of a sinking ship in the twilight of his career. With less than two months to go, the route for the race had not yet been announced, and the future looked bleak. Torriani initially put up the money himself, and it took a miracle of diplomacy to get RAI, the national broadcaster, to commit to the event without there being a main sponsor or money from the event's owners, before a stroke of luck brought Coca-Cola on board, as they were launching a new drink in Italy at the time. That might seem like a quaint story from the past, about a passionate race director somehow pulling the event out of a seemingly terminal nosedive, but the same menacing spectre still looms large in a sport that in some ways is less financially secure than ever. There is more money, sure, and a much bigger audience, but the costs have snowballed, too.

'From my point of view, cycling has created a lot of new costs, but it hasn't been able to make the pie any bigger. In terms of expense, it's not at the level of football, but it's not like it was 20 years ago either. And there's a difference, an important imbalance with sponsors, because with some exceptions, if they invest in a team, they do it for a specific amount of time. Most of them for four or five years, there have only been four or five names who've backed a team for 20 years.

'Compared with football, the major difference is that it's more stable. The team structure is stronger, and the sponsor is a client. With cycling, the team is a client. OK, they might be registered companies, but the reality is that without that sponsor, they don't exist. I think we need to reduce some of the costs because if they don't have decent revenue, the costs can kill a team.

'As for Italy, we need to invest more in the sport, but that's not to criticise the Federation, that's a business too with a balance sheet and a requirement not to be in the red. If you look at something like a track programme, running all year, with a covered track and everything that goes with it, it costs a lot. I don't know how much the others spend, but obviously the economic problems here in recent years have affected that ability.

'It would be important to invest, but to do that you need resources. Trying to manage the events and employees, and it's not as if there are a lot of revenue streams for something like a national federation. You might find a big sponsor for the national team jersey, but after that? What is someone going to do, sponsor the press conference? But how much would it cost to do everything that a federation has to, on the track and the road, with youngsters, with all the coaches. I don't know any of the figures involved, but it would make you tired just thinking about it.

'Here in Italy, it's been 10 or 15 years of financial difficulty for the country, so everyone feels that. The Giro and our other races continue to attract interest, but it's hard work. So even if we're doing well, it's a lot more difficult than it used to be. The needs of companies change; when there isn't money, the first thing they cut is marketing. But we've come out of it well and there's hope that we can continue to improve.'

Developments have been positive since the turn of the last decade. In a broader sense, the sport has finally come to terms with the doping scandals and flagrant dereliction of the rules that dogged it during the 1990s and into the new millennium. And closer to home, the Giro seems to have rediscovered its form after several years in the doldrums. Gone are the inhumane stages that many hold at least partially accountable for the proliferation of performance-enhancing drugs, the senselessly long transfers between stage finishes and the following day's start and, for the most part, the race closures that hurt the sport's appeal at a more local level. Reversing the trend of a decade ago, RCS are now reinvigorating storied old events and creating new races such as the Strade Bianche spring classic that has captured the imagination of riders and fans alike. A calendar full of events might not directly affect the Giro d'Italia, which, after a century has become something of a national institution, but they are invaluable in terms of creating interest among the wider public, framing the annual spectacle and giving a new generation of tifosi something to engage with from February to October.

'A great Giro needs to be a synthesis of all of the disciplines,' offers the director, as the conversation turns to the race's rediscovered humanity. 'There needs to be the right mix, so I will never think of doing 15 mountain stages. It would be easy for me to design a race from Sicily to the Dolomites, up through the Apennines, only in the mountains. But there need to be sprints, time trials, and the mountains, with climbs that are sufficient to bring out the best rider.

'One of the things I've tried to do in recent years is to give the Giro a more human scale. Shorter transfers, for example, more attention to the riders, so that they don't race 130 kilometres and then spend the night driving 200 kilometres. Extremism doesn't do anyone any good.'

Another kind of extremism threatened to cripple cycling in the past 20 years: the use of performance-enhancing drugs. And while Vegni, like any sensible veteran of professional sport, stops short of saying that it's totally clean, he is hopeful for the future in terms of ensuring competition on a level playing field.

'They were dark years, to tell you the truth, not just because you couldn't trust the performances or the results, they were dark years because cycling passed every limit. Not only sporting boundaries, but also every limit that the human physique could bear. It arrived at the point where people were risking their lives.

'It was a battle. Now, with more knowledge, a new generation of riders, much stronger testing, it's shown that it's no longer so easy to avoid controls. It's become more difficult, you can't just get drugs from anywhere. They're still there, in my opinion, but the use is more and more limited. It's not possible any more to have a big performance development, like 20 years ago.

'Maybe in 20 years we'll be saying another thing, but I think that the controls we have today were born thanks to that period. That era taught us that what we were doing was inadequate. There needed to be scientific research, too, to understand what we were dealing with. Maybe it's still not 100 per cent, but I believe we've already done a lot. We have surprise testing, controls outside of races, the biological passport – all of these things are strong deterrents. Beforehand, they took the blood and urine from the winner and that was it.

'There are different interpretations, but doping was born in those years [the 1990s]. We're talking about cycling here, but those drugs fuelled a lot of other types of athletes too. That's important to say.

'If you look at the number of controls and the number of positive findings, you'd see that cycling is not the "top" sport of dopers. We do a lot of tests, and in percentage terms it's obvious that you're going to find one. If you only did two tests and they were both doped, that's another story. That's not to say we're better than anyone else, we've had our own iniquities, but now everyone is aware that we're doing something different and people are starting to believe again.'

At this point, he returns to financial insecurity, which Vegni believes is both at the root of the sport's recent problems, and the main threat to its immediate future.

'There's always one idiot on duty,' he says to the possibility of someone doping today. 'That's human nature, but it's also because the system doesn't guarantee anything. I've always said that, if a new rider had the possibility of a contract of at least two years, it would give them the chance to adapt to a new environment and then to express themselves, perhaps there wouldn't be the need to demonstrate something immediately.

'Today, they give them a six-month trial contract, and if it doesn't go well, they send you home. Imagine the work that the kid has to go through to arrive to that point, and just like that, they can burn all his hopes. That's another aspect of the problem.

'I can understand the teams as well, the contracts cost money, so we're back to the old discussion of the pie. If I have a budget that allows me to give two kids contracts for two years, I'd do it, but the problem is that I don't have the money, so I have to save, and the perception is that if the young guy doesn't go well right away, he's not worth it. But maybe he just didn't settle right away and so he stumbled.'

Another regrettable change – and surely a thorn in the paw of any race director – is the way in which modern riders approach the race calendar. Gone are the days when someone like Bernard Hinault would go swashbuckling his way across the continent from early spring until late autumn, as adept at laying waste to the opposition in the muddy, early-season classics as he was at trouncing everyone in the mountains of a grand tour. And in Vegni's eyes, at least, it seems as if most of the current crop are failing to live up to their billing.

'I can only speak of the riders I've seen,' he says, talking of favourites. 'The Eddy Merckx I knew was at the end of his career. I started working in this world in 1976, which if I'm right was the last Giro that Felice Gimondi won … I struggle with the dates! I wouldn't want to talk about them, it's better to talk about what I've seen, from Francesco Moser's generation, Roger De Vlaeminck and all those guys.

'I think that there's probably been one emblematic rider for every decade. And every decade represents a different kind of cycling, so to say who the best was would be impossible.

'The riders who you have to mention: Miguel Indurain, Bernard Hinault, and for all that he could have been you couldn't leave out Pantani. Of the last decade, I think the best rider has been Alberto Contador. These were all riders who could win everything, but more than that, they were good men, polite and sincere.

'Of course, I've had much more contact with Alberto, and for me he's an exceptional rider, a serious person who whenever he said, "Mauro, I'm not coming," he didn't come and when he said, "Mauro, I'll be there," he came even when the team didn't want him to.

'Someone who's on the right road today, for me, is Vincenzo Nibali. He has demonstrated that he can win everywhere – the Giro, the Vuelta, the Tour – one of only six to do it. And he's won Lombardia! Every year, at Milano–Sanremo he attacks on the Poggio, OK, he doesn't win, but he's there. From February to October, he races. I think if you ask me in 10 years, he'll be on the list.

'I don't have any others to add. Forget about that guy who won seven Tours! There was too little humanity in that for me. I'm talking about the programming, let's not talk about what he did or didn't have, just in terms of the racing, a champion needs to demonstrate that he can win everywhere. You can't just have one object a year and aim for that and win that. OK, so you're strong there, but in the arch of a year, what kind of a performance is that?

'Even in Vincenzo's bad year, 2015, he tried everywhere – and then he finished the year winning Lombardia, a Monument, which is no small achievement. That's a champion. That's why I rate Hinault and Contador, because everywhere they went they showed that they were really strong, real racers.

'Riders who basically do one race a year don't excite me. Hinault won the Worlds, won classics, we're not even talking about the same thing any more. And now, someone wins only one event, and we're supposed to put them in the same category as someone like that? A great rider can't finish his career without winning a Giro, or at least trying to. Or vice versa, not to speak only about the others, if an Italian is supposed to be strong, but he only wins the Giro and never the Tour? They need to compete in all of the races at the top level. And I have my doubts about anyone who doesn't.

'As for when people ask me, "Who are you bringing to the Giro?" I need patience to respond. Whoever doesn't come to the Giro is missing out, it's not the Giro that is losing. It's the Giro that makes champions, the Tour that makes champions, not the other way around.'

One thing that hasn't changed since before Vegni's time is also, perhaps, the most distinctive trait of the sport in the twenty-first century, and one that gives him plenty of cause for optimism as the Giro approaches its 100th edition. Bike racing, for all its problems and its myriad flaws, remains a sport of the people, and even now, in an ever-more micro-managed environment, its greatest dramas continue to play out on open roads, inches from the fans, without a ticket or a turnstile in sight. As long as the Giro stays true to that principle, it will have a place in the hearts of Italians, and of race fans around the world.

'Cycling, even in the darkest moments, had the fortitude to hold on to the public,' muses Vegni, our conversation drawing to a close. 'Its capacity to be close to its fans has been the sport's greatest strength. Some people might say that it's a sport for old people, a sport of sweat and of mud, not something attractive, that it has just become the new golf ... For me, in those moments, cycling still has the power to overcome those crises and the impasses, only because of its ability to keep its protagonists close to the people.

'The riders who stop to talk to kids and to sign autographs, the way that people can go to the start and put their hand on the back of someone like Vincenzo Nibali. That's what makes this sport special. Tell me another sport that has that, where the public, the real public, not a selected few or those who pay, has the opportunity to shake hands, talk, take a selfie with a star.

'Cycling isn't the biggest sport in the world, but it is one of the most important, and we're talking about the very best athletes. What other sport gives you that possibility? It doesn't call you to the stadium; it comes to you. And it doesn't just show you athletes, it shows you so much of the country, that would otherwise be difficult to come to know. These are great values that no one can take away. That is cycling's great virtue.'

That unique ability to twist its way through a country, into its culture, slow enough to touch the thousands it passes every day, and yet fast enough to excite the millions watching at home. Mauro Vegni's route for the 2017 Giro d'Italia was a tribute to that virtue, and a testimony to his belief that the great stage races should show you all of the country, revealing hidden treasures and uncovering the roads less ridden. Three days on the island of Sardinia, then across the Tyrrhenian Sea for another two stages in Sicily. From there, another ferry across the Strait of Messina to the mainland, so close you can see it, only a few kilometres in the distance, and yet, in so many ways, a world away. Calabria, Basilicata, Puglia, into the tiny province of Molise, on to Abruzzo, inland, to the Apennine Mountains, heading north, up the craggy spine of the peninsula, through Umbria and into Tuscany and Emilia-Romagna, before a final gruelling week in the race's most familiar territories, the mountainous north, the peaks of Piemonte, Lombardy, Alto Adige, Friuli-Venezia Giulia, and Veneto.

Logistically, it would be ill-advised to attempt such an ambitious cartographic enterprise every year, but once in a while, it's a worthy aspiration and a grand thing to see up close. Because only the Giro could weave a thread strong enough to stitch 15 of Italy's 20 contrastive regions together and make sense of it all. And regardless of the racing, those excursions to rarely visited shores always lend events a little touch of historical significance.

The previous time that the race had started in Sardinia, in 2007, the sport was very different, still doing its best to pretend that the likes of Alessandro Petacchi and Danilo Di Luca were clean, and that the 23-year-old Riccardo Riccò was just fresh-faced and full of promise (and who knows what else), a full four years away from his DIY blood transfusion and the ensuing kidney failure, hospitalisation, and ridicule. The time before that, in 1991, a 24-year-old Mario Cipollini took the sprint in Cagliari, the island's capital, just the fourth of an eventual 42 stage wins at the Giro. Davide Cassani, the current Italian national team manager, was still half a decade away from retirement. The only other time that the Giro visited, for a single stage in 1961, Jacques Anquetil was in his pomp, Fausto Coppi was only dead a year, and Bertha Mae LeMond was pregnant in the United States with a son who would grow up to leave an indelible mark on cycling. It was still six months before Brian Epstein would first meet the Beatles, the US Bay of Pigs invasion of Cuba had failed to oust Fidel Castro from power the previous month, and Harper Lee was just awarded the Pulitzer Prize for her novel *To Kill a Mockingbird*. Two days after the race left Cagliari for Marsala in western Sicily, John F. Kennedy told a joint session of Congress in Washington DC that he wanted to send a man to the moon. What's all this got to do with the Giro? Not a lot, perhaps. Or maybe everything. The point is that the 2017 route was a rare rare thing. Almost half the race in the Mezzogiorno, contradicting the stereotype that Italian cycling exists only in the north, and bringing the country's biggest annual event to people all too often isolated or excluded from the nation's premier occasions. There were grumbles at the beginning from some corners of the press room – too many stages for the sprinters with little else on the road to spark the imagination – but that argument held little water amongst the throngs of fans strung out along the roads in sparsely populated and often forgotten interior of Sardinia, or the excited masses that gathered hours before the day's stage had even begun to enjoy the warm, sparkling promise of summer, contrasting the black, volcanic ash of Mount Etna's upper slopes with an abundance of colourful flags and banners. The Corsa Rosa, Vegni might say, belongs to them too, even if they so rarely get to be a part of it.

The Grande Partenza was dealt two blows before any of the riders had even arrived in the appealing coastal town of Alghero, where the race begun on 5 May. A crash in April deprived the locals of the event's biggest draw, Fabio Aru, Italian cycling's great hope and, with the exception of the great Gianfranco Zola, the island's most famous sportsman. Aru is the obvious successor to Vincenzo Nibali, Sicilian, another islander, who rode with the young Sardinian on the Astana team for three years, during which time Aru developed from a young prospect, known to the cognoscenti, to a grand tour winner in his own right. At 26, this was to be his Giro; he'd already made the podium twice, won stages at the Giro and the Tour de France, and taken the general classification in what was an exhilarating edition of the Vuelta a España in 2015.

Unhappier still, his replacement as the Astana leader for the Giro, the vivacious and universally popular Michele Scarponi, was tragically killed in a collision with a van, close to his home in Filottrano, near the Adriatic coast, while on a training ride on 22 April. The Marchigiano, as the natives of the Marche region are known, was retroactively declared the winner of the 2011 Giro following Alberto Contador's disqualification, but had been a divisive character himself earlier in his career, serving bans for his involvement in the Operación Puerto doping scandal and then later for admitting links to the controversial doctor Michele Ferrari. Later in his career, however, Scarponi's personality and the selfless way in which he rode for his leaders – Vincenzo Nibali, for one, owes his 2016 title in no small part to his late friend – endeared him overwhelmingly to the Italian public, and even with a minority who were slow to forgive his previous sins, to a large part of cycling's global fanbase, too.

Even so, the field that lined up at the start in Alghero was one of the best in recent memory at the Giro, and even after crashes and illnesses in the early stages removed Geraint Thomas, Mikel Landa, Steven Kruijswijk, and Adam Yates from GC contention, it was obvious from early on that the tifosi were in for a treat. The route's focus on balance – a mixture of shorter stages to exciting uphill finishes, long time trials and a handful of brutally hard days in the Alps and the Dolomites – made for fantastic racing. And the absence of a dominant team, or one domineering talent, made for one of the closest and captivating grand tours in years.

Of the favourites, none were impervious. Nairo Quintana began the race talking of a Giro-Tour double, but was never quite his inspirational best in the mountains. Vincenzo Nibali brought the racing nous and daring style that's served him so well in the past, but was with a new, disjointed team and some way off his best form physically. France's great hope, Thibaut Pinot, was certainly worth considering, but his best grand tour result had been third at the Tour in 2014, when he finished more than eight minutes behind Nibali. While Tom Dumoulin, the young, powerful Dutchman who'd impressed so much in the 2016 edition, and who had looked capable of denying Aru that Vuelta win until the race entered its final days, wasn't supposed to be capable of of hanging on in the high mountains.

Few could have predicted what eventually transpired. Dumoulin, visibly leaner than in previous seasons but seemingly every bit as powerful against the clock, surprised everyone with his abilities in the mountains. With his lighter rivals nipping at his heels, and Quintana trying his best to launch a trademark attack in the final kilometres, the Dutchman refused to crack on Blockhaus, central Italy's most revered mountain, where Eddy Merckx took his first grand tour stage win, half a century past. And then, Stage 14, from the home of Fausto Coppi to Oropa, the scene of what was perhaps Marco Pantani's last truly happy moment on the bike, he produced a victory that was more impressive than that of Il Pirata in '99. Not as frantic, not as demonstrative, but then, (we'd hope) not doped, either. All that from someone who's a relative giant in compared to the little Colombian that he beat. Dumoulin left Quintana in his dust with a forceful, confident sprint in the final metres, the kind of display that the leader's jersey deserves, but all too seldom gets. That stage win put him 02' 47' ahead of Quintana, and almost another minute ahead of Pinot and Nibali, meaning they'd need to steal at least five minutes from him in the final week. Not impossible, by any measure, but Dumoulin was a different rider to the one who had fallen apart in the final stages of the 2015 Vuelta, and shaking him in the mountains was not going to be easy.

Nibali's emphatic victory on the Queen Stage to Bormio was a thing of beauty, and the perfect illustration of why the Sicilian is a jewel that we should all treasure, but it was too little, too late. Because even though he took the day's honours, in the grander scheme of things, that afternoon in northern Lombardy was to be Dumoulin's denouement. Having been knocking on the door for years now, the Maastricht native proved that he was more than just a good time triallist, and that even though he comes from a country that is mostly at or below sea level, he is at home at altitude – and more than capable of dealing with pressure. That was something he'd already shown earlier in the race, letting his lighter adversaries ride their own race on the tougher gradients as he paced himself to the summit, sure in his own abilities. Which is easier said than done, because at that moment, seeing a rival disappear around the bend on a hellish climb, when you're at your limit and losing time, must be excruciating.

It takes a cool head to know that you can manage losses and make up time elsewhere. Even after that now infamous nature break, when a miscalculation in Dumoulin's dietary regimen resulted in him having to stop on the side of the road to relieve himself, he refused to panic, limiting his losses with a heroic ascent of the Stelvio, and, fighting against a barrage of vicious cramps, holding his own on the final kilometres as Nibali, a peerless descender, drilled the downhill. And all that, after two weeks of defying the forecasts, and riding against the coming tide of uphill finishes. Having overcome that double-ascent of the Stelvio, Dumoulin could really begin to dream, and not even Stage 19, where he lost a minute and the Maglia Rosa to Quintana, could dull the edge of his optimism.

The final stage, a time trial from the famous motor racing track in Monza to downtown Milan, had Quintana, Dumoulin, Pinot, and Nibali all within a minute of one another. In terms of spectacle, it wasn't quite Greg LeMond and Laurent Fignon at the '89 Tour, but it wasn't far off. A poorly judged corner or an unfortunate puncture could have handed the victory to any of the quartet, and so it wasn't until Quintana, hopelessly clinging to hopes for a second Giro GC win, turned from Piazza San

Babila and onto the tight, business-like thoroughfare of Corso Giacomo Matteotti, with a kilometre to go, that Dumoulin knew for sure. He was the first Dutchman to win the Giro d'Italia, and the man to end a cycling-mad nation's 37-year desperate wait for a grand tour victory. On the 28 May 2017, he joined a very exclusive club of three, with Joop Zoetemelk, who won the Vuelta in 1979 and the Tour in 1980, and the stylish world champion of 1964, Jan Janssen, who won in Spain in '67 and in France the year after.

With only 40 seconds separating Dumoulin from Nibali in third, it was the second-closest podium in Giro history, the gap just marginally wider than in 1974, when the final result saw Eddy Merckx 12 seconds ahead of Gianbattista Baronchelli and 33 ahead of Felice Gimondi. It was also only the third time that the Maglia Rosa had changed hands in the final stage, the other two occasions being 1984, when Francesco Moser denied Laurent Fignon, and 2012, when Ryder Hesjedal overcame Joaquim Rodríguez in the final TT.

None of that will have concerned Dumoulin, who was, at the finish line, caught up in what he could only describe as a crazy feeling. He admitted to struggling to stay calm, and to thinking the worst when he saw the early time splits on the big screen. As he told a huddled mass of journalists: 'You're never sure of winning. You always doubt.

'I'm not the first TT rider who can do well in the mountains. Miguel Indurain is five steps ahead of me. There are guys like Bradley Wiggins, but I don't want to compare myself to anyone. It's just an amazing day. I'm really happy. [And] I was never a bad climber. I always had that in me.'

Off the record and over a beer, one of his fellow riders put it a little more bluntly. 'Tom's just an incredible rider,' he said, smiling. 'I mean, he stopped to take a shit and he still won the race. What more can you say?'

ACKNOWLEDGEMENTS

This book wouldn't have been possible without the help of many friends, family members and colleagues along the way, and even though there are too many to thank here, some deserve particular mention. My agent Kevin Pocklington was invaluable from the beginning, and I was very grateful for his composure and his common sense during a couple of difficult moments that might otherwise have been my undoing. I'm also indebted to James Spackman, Penny Daniel, and everyone at Profile Books for their enthusiasm and support from the very start – and for their patience with me towards the end. And Susanne Hillen deserves plenty of credit for her editing and advice; she made this a better book.

It's a testament to the nature of this sport that of all the managers, directors, and riders, both past and present, whom I contacted while researching this book, every single one was incredibly generous with their time. The same is true of Mauro Vegni and his team at RCS Sport; a nicer group of people you will not find, and given the stressful environment in which they work, that's saying something. In addition, I need to thank

Manolo Bertocchi and Stefano Diciatteo for their help over the years, because without their assistance and their cooperation, my work wouldn't be possible.

Lastly, special thanks to my friend Guy Andrews, who gave me a chance early on and found space for my rambling in a publication filled with better talents. Oh, and to the photographer Paolo Ciaberta, for always driving the car and for never being boring at dinner.

LIST OF WINNERS

Year	Nationality	Rider	Team
2017	Netherlands	DUMOULIN Tom	Sunweb
2016	Italy	NIBALI Vincenzo	Astana
2015	Spain	CONTADOR Alberto	Tinkoff-Saxo
2014	Colombia	QUINTANA Nairo	Movistar Team
2013	Italy	NIBALI Vincenzo	Astana
2012	Canada	HESJEDAL Ryder	Garmin-Barracuda
2011	Italy	SCARPONI Michele	Lampre-Isd
2010	Italy	BASSO Ivan	Liquigas-Doimo
2009	Russian Federation	MENCHOV Denis	Rabobank
2008	Spain	CONTADOR Alberto	Astana
2007	Italy	DI LUCA Danilo	Liquigas
2006	Italy	BASSO Ivan	Csc
2005	Italy	SAVOLDELLI Paolo	Discovery Channel
2004	Italy	CUNEGO Damiano	Saeco
2003	Italy	SIMONI Gilberto	Saeco
2002	Italy	SAVOLDELLI Paolo	Index-Alexia
2001	Italy	SIMONI Gilberto	Lampre-Daikin
2000	Italy	GARZELLI Stefano	Mercatone Uno Albacom
1999	Italy	GOTTI Ivan	Team Polti
1998	Italy	PANTANI Marco	Mercatone Uno-Bianchi

Year	Nationality	Rider	Team
1997	Italy	GOTTI Ivan	Saeco
1996	Russian Federation	TONKOV Pavel	Panaria-Vinavil
1995	Switzerland	ROMINGER Tony	Mapei-Gb
1994	Russian Federation	BERZIN Eugeni	Gewiss-Ballan
1993	Spain	INDURAIN Miguel	Banesto
1992	Spain	INDURAIN Miguel	Banesto
1991	Italy	CHIOCCIOLI Franco	Del Tongo M.G.
1990	Italy	BUGNO Gianni	Chateau d'Ax
1989	France	FIGNON Laurent	System U
1988	USA	HAMPSTEN Andrew	Seven Eleven Hoonved
1987	Ireland	ROCHE Stephen	Carrera
1986	Italy	VISENTINI Roberto	Carrera
1985	France	HINAULT Bernard	La Vie Claire-Look
1984	Italy	MOSER Francesco	Gis Tuc-Lu
1983	Italy	SARONNI Giuseppe	Del Tongo-Colnago
1982	France	HINAULT Bernard	Renault-Elf-Gitane
1981	Italy	BATTAGLIN Giovanni	Inoxpran
1980	France	HINAULT Bernard	Renault-Gitane
1979	Italy	SARONNI Giuseppe	Scic-Bottecchia
1978	Belgium	DE MUYNCK Johan	Bianchi-Faema
1977	Belgium	POLLENTIER Michel	Fiandria
1976	Italy	GIMONDI Felice	Bianchi-Campagnolo
1975	Italy	BERTOGLIO Fausto	Jollyceramica
1974	Belgium	MERCKX Eddy	Molteni
1973	Belgium	MERCKX Eddy	Molteni
1972	Belgium	MERCKX Eddy	Molteni
1971	Sweden	PETTERSON Gösta	Ferretti
1970	Belgium	MERCKX Eddy	Faemino
1969	Italy	GIMONDI Felice	Salvarani
1968	Belgium	MERCKX Eddy	Faema
1967	Italy	GIMONDI Felice	Salvarani
1966	Italy	MOTTA Gianni	Molteni
1965	Italy	ADORNI Vittorio	Salvarani
1964	France	ANQUETIL Jacques	St. Raphael
1963	Italy	BALMAMION Franco	Carpano

Year	Nationality	Rider	Team
1962	Italy	BALMAMION Franco	Carpano
1961	Italy	PAMBIANCO Arnaldo	Fides
1960	France	ANQUETIL Jacques	Fynsec
1959	Luxembourg	GAUL Charly	Emi-Guerra
1958	Italy	BALDINI Ercole	Legnano
1957	Italy	NENCINI Gastone	Chlorodont
1956	Luxembourg	GAUL Charly	Guerra
1955	Italy	MAGNI Fiorenzo	Nivea-Fuchs
1954	Switzerland	CLERICI Carlo	Guerra-Svizzera
1953	Italy	COPPI Fausto	Bianchi
1952	Italy	COPPI Fausto	Bianchi
1951	Italy	MAGNI Fiorenzo	Ganna
1950	Switzerland	KOBLET Hugo	Guerra-Svizzera
1949	Italy	COPPI Fausto	Bianchi
1948	Italy	MAGNI Fiorenzo	Wilier Triestina
1947	Italy	COPPI Fausto	Bianchi
1946	Italy	BARTALI Gino	Legnano
1940	Italy	COPPI Fausto	Legnano
1939	Italy	VALETTI Giovanni	Frejus
1938	Italy	VALETTI Giovanni	Frejus
1937	Italy	BARTALI Gino	Legnano
1936	Italy	BARTALI Gino	Legnano
1935	Italy	BERGAMASCHI Vasco	Maino
1934	Italy	GUERRA Learco	Maino
1933	Italy	BINDA Alfredo	Legnano
1932	Italy	PESENTI Antonio	Wolsit
1931	Italy	CAMUSSO Francesco	Gloria
1930	Italy	MARCHISIO Luigi	Legnano
1929	Italy	BINDA Alfredo	Legnano
1928	Italy	BINDA Alfredo	Wolsit
1927	Italy	BINDA Alfredo	Legnano
1926	Italy	BRUNERO Giovanni	Legnano
1925	Italy	BINDA Alfredo	Legnano
1924	Italy	ENRICI Giuseppe	Legnano
1923	Italy	GIRARDENGO Costante	Maino

Year	Nationality	Rider	Team
1922	Italy	BRUNERO Giovanni	Legnano
1921	Italy	BRUNERO Giovanni	Legnano
1920	Italy	BELLONI Gaetano	Bianchi
1919	Italy	GIRARDENGO Costante	Stucchi
1914	Italy	CALZOLARI Alfonso	Stucchi
1913	Italy	ORIANI Carlo	Maino
1912	Italy	ATALA (team event)	Atala
1911	Italy	GALETTI Carlo	Bianchi
1910	Italy	GALETTI Carlo	Atala
1909	Italy	GANNA Luigi	Atala

LIST OF ILLUSTRATIONS

1. 'Viva Coppi' pennant from 1954

2. Crowds in Florence's Parco delle Cascine welcoming the first edition of the race, 1909 ©2006 Alinari/TopFoto

3. The front page of the *Gazzetta dello Sport*, 24 August 1908, announcing the inaugural Giro d'Italia ©RCS Sport/*La Gazzetta dello Sport*

4. Armando Cougnet, the first Patron of the Giro, was only 18 years old when he joined the editorial staff of the *Gazzetta* in 1898

5. Luigi Ganna with Carlo Galetti, May 1909 ©akg-images/ Fototeca Gilardi

6. Alfredo Binda with Emilio Colombo, the editor of the *Gazzetta dello Sport*

7. Luigi Ganna, Eberardo Pavesi, Giovanni Micheletto, Carlo Galetti and Natale Bosco pictured during the 1912 Giro ©MARKA/Alamy Stock Photo

8. The Bersaglieri ©Museo Centrale del Risorgimento/ Mondadori Portfolio via Getty Images

9. Costante Girardengo, one of the first truly rich professional athletes ©MARKA/Alamy Stock Photo

10. Alfredo Binda, often known as il *Trombettiere di Cittiglio* ©akg-images

11. Giovanni Brunero was the first rider to win the Giro three times, in 1921, 1922, and 1926 ©Olycom SPA/REX/Shutterstock

12. Learco Guerra, the man they called 'The Human Locomotive' ©Olycom SPA/REX/Shutterstock

13. Alfonsina Strada competing in the 1924 edition ©akg-images/Interfoto/Friedrich

14. Ottavio Bottecchia became the first Italian to win the Tour de France ©Olycom SPA/REX/Shutterstock

15. Fausto Coppi with Giulia Occhini and their son, Angelo Fausto ©Mondadori Portfolio via Getty Images

16. Gino Bartali and Fausto Coppi in many ways represented the contrasting faces of a rapidly changing country ©Olycom SPA/REX/Shutterstock

17. Eddie Merckx, known as 'The Cannibal', on the infamous Passo dello Stelvio ©Fotoreporter Sirotti

18. Fiorenzo Magni, Italy's 'Third Man', here steering his bike with his teeth, having refused to retire from the 1956 race with a broken clavicle ©Alinari/TopFoto

19. Francesco Moser was the favourite of Italian cycling fans everywhere

20. Giuseppe Saronni was also one of the dominant Giro stars of his generation ©Olycom SPA/REX/Shutterstock

21. Roberto Visentini, a gifted rider and the champion of the 1986 Giro ©Fotoreporter Sirotti

22. Stephen Roche, pictured with Roberto Conti, Johan van der Velde and Robert Millar ©Fotoreporter Sirotti

23. The 7-Eleven team ©Fotoreporter Sirotti

24. 7-Eleven's Andy Hampsten in appalling conditions over the Passo di Gavia © Cor Vos

25. Miguel Indurain pictured with Claudio Chiappucci and Franco Chioccioli during the 1993 Giro ©Olycom SPA/REX/Shutterstock

26. Paolo Savoldelli earned the nickname Il Falco, 'The Falcon' ©Str/Epa/REX/Shutterstock

27. Marco Pantani was loved for his impulsiveness, his daring, and his sense of the theatrical ©Olycom SPA/REX/Shutterstock

28. Spain's Alberto Contador remains one of the most popular riders in the peloton among Italian race fans ©REUTERS/Alessandro Garofalo

29. Vincenzo Nibali gave one of the most extraordinary individual performances in recent years to win on the frozen slops of the Tre Cime di Lavaredo, RB/Cor Vos © 2013

INDEX